All Scripture references taken from the KJV of the Holy Bible, unless otherwise indicated.

NOT FORSAKEN OR FORGOTTEN

by Dr. Marlene Miles

Freshwater Press 2026

Freshwaterpress9@gmail.com

ISBN: 978-1-971933-35-1

Paperback Version

Table of Contents

NOT FORSAKEN OR FORGOTTEN

Never will I leave you;

never will I forsake you. **(Hebrews 13:5)**

Abandoned

In the Bible, how someone treats the weak, aged, widowed, or dependent is a direct measure of their righteousness. That includes elderly mothers, aging wives, widows, and women whose value is no longer being *extracted.*

God watches this closely.

Abandonment of the aged is treated as *wickedness*. There is a repeated Biblical category of sin that includes abandoning parents, neglecting widows, casting off aging spouses, benefiting from someone's youth or strength and discarding them later

Do not despise your mother when she is old. (Proverbs 23:22)

That verse wouldn't exist if this were not already happening.

God explicitly positions Himself as Defender of those people

A father to the fatherless, a defender of widows, is God in His holy dwelling. *Psalm* 68:5

When humans abandon, God steps in as legal protector — which means someone else is now on the wrong side of Him. That's why prayers "against" abandonment are actually appeals to God's justice; they are not curses.

The woman-specific emphasis is not accidental. Scripture repeatedly highlights women because, historically and practically, women outlive men. Women often sacrifice earning years for caregiving. women can become economically vulnerable later in life. Women are more likely to be discarded when aging.

God rebukes men for treachery against "the wife of your youth (Malachi 2:15–16). That is devastatingly specific. The sin is not divorce alone — the sin is discarding a woman after benefiting from her prime years.

God calls it *treachery*.

In the New Testament, abandonment becomes a faith issue.

Anyone who does not provide for their relatives… has denied the faith and is worse than an unbeliever. *1 Timothy* 5:8

That is one of the strongest condemnations in the New Testament, and it's about neglect, not theology. So, when someone prays against people abandoning aging mothers or wives, they are praying against a behavior that Scripture already condemns harshly.

Why would someone pray *against* it? Because abandonment creates generational trauma, poverty, bitterness, premature death and spiritual injustice. In

Biblical terms, abandonment releases a curse-like consequence, because covenant was broken.

The prayer is often saying, in effect, "God, do not allow people to prosper through betrayal. Do not allow someone to consume love, labor, youth, and sacrifice — and then walk away untouched." Don't let them use me up, Lord, in the Name of Jesus.

That is a justice prayer, not a revenge prayer.

This book sits at the intersection of covenant theology, gender justice, aging and dignity, family responsibility, and judgment and Mercy. What's in this book is often deep inside teachings on widows, teachings on honor, teachings on covenant, and teachings on judgment. Rarely is it named plainly. I'm plainly naming it and it doesn't have to be about a widow or an old person.

A prayer against leaving the wife of one's youth, or not being the victim of such abandonment is not necessarily a cry for justice.

No.

A cry for justice is not automatically a judgmental prayer.

It depends on the posture.

There's a difference between "Lord, make this right." And "Lord, punish them because I am right." One is appeal. The other is accusation.

Biblically, cries for justice are everywhere. The Psalms are full of them. "How long, O Lord?" "Vindicate me." "Rise up and judge the Earth."

Those are not petty. They are covenantal appeals. They assume there *is* a moral order. God sees. God weighs. God responds. That is not judgmental; that is faith in justice.

A prayer becomes judgmental when it demands a specific punishment. It assumes full knowledge of motives. It centers ego instead of righteousness. It refuses Mercy as an option. But a cry for justice that says: "God, you see this. I trust you to handle it." — that is surrender, not self-righteousness.

A woman praying, "Lord, do not let me be discarded in my old age" is not judging anyone. She is asking for covenant fidelity. That's not revenge, that's longing for righteousness. The diagnostic question is: Does the prayer end with "and let Your will be done," or does it end with "and let them pay"?

Not Forsaken or Forgotten

There are prayers people pray because they are afraid. Then there are prayers people pray because they have finally named something that should never have been normalized. This book was born from the second kind.

I once heard a minister pray—briefly, almost in passing—against people being left when they are old. Mothers. Wives. Women whose strength had already been poured out elsewhere. The prayer itself was striking, but what lingered was not what he said—it was what he did not say.

The focus was placed on those who might be abandoned, as though the primary spiritual work belonged to the vulnerable: *pray this does not happen to you*. Little was said about the responsibility of those who leave. Less was said about loyalty. Almost nothing was said about accountability.

This book spawned from that prayer that should have been explained, and to all those who find themselves alone, not by choice, or through no wrongdoing on their part, remembering that none of us are perfect. Why is there silence around abandonment protects the wrong people, so I wrote this book for those who may have found themselves abandoned or forgotten, at any time, but, especially later in life.

Scripture does not ask the vulnerable to prevent betrayal. Scripture commands the strong not to commit it. The Bible does not treat aging as failure. If you think about it, aging is success. It sure beats the alternative. The Bible does not frame diminished strength as disqualification. It never assigns moral responsibility to the person who was left alone.

Instead, Scripture consistently places responsibility on the one who walks away. To be forsaken is not simply to be alone. It is to be abandoned by someone who had an obligation to remain. To be forgotten is not memory loss—it is erasure after benefit has already been received.

God is explicit: He is neither.

This book is not written to teach women how to remain "valuable enough" to keep loyalty. It is not written to help people pray their way out of being betrayed. And it is not written to spiritualize what Scripture plainly calls treachery.

It is written to name a sin that many, including the modern church often avoids because it is uncomfortable, inconvenient, and implicates people who prefer to be affirmed rather than corrected.

We live in a culture that upgrades phones, replaces cars, and quietly applies the same logic to people. Youth is prized. Productivity is rewarded. Beauty is leveraged. And when those currencies diminish, loyalty is suddenly treated as optional.

Scripture rejects this logic outright. Covenant assumes time. It assumes aging. It assumes seasons when nothing is returned. That is not a flaw in covenant—it is the point. When Scripture speaks of widows, aging mothers, and the wife of one's youth, it is not being sentimental. It is being judicial. God identifies Himself as Defender precisely because He knows how easily the strong justify leaving the weak.

This book is written to restore moral weight where it belongs. It speaks to husbands who confuse desire with permission. To children who confuse distance with exemption. To communities that confuse silence with peace. And to churches that confuse neutrality with Grace.

It also speaks to those who fear being left—not to tell them how to prevent it, but to tell them the truth: If people fail, God does not. If covenant is broken, He records it. If loyalty is honored, He remembers it.

You are not disposable because time has passed. You are not forgotten because usefulness has changed. And you are not forsaken simply because someone chose betrayal over faithfulness.

This is not a book of accusation. It is a book of alignment--, aligning with the God who sees, remembers, and judges rightly.

> Every wise woman buildeth her house: but the foolish plucketh it down with her hands. (Proverbs 14:1)

NOT FORSAKEN OR FORGOTTEN is not a reassurance whispered to the abandoned, it is a declaration spoken before Heaven and Earth. Loyalty still matters. Covenant still binds. No one is invisible to God—especially not the ***Leavers***. They are the ones who find it easy to leave if they are 'not happy', bored, uncomfortable, or no longer want responsibility.

Be sure though, that you are a wise woman and not tearing down your own house. Walk upright; stay prayerful. God will see to the rest.

If you are one who has been building and building this book is for you. If you've been building a life and building people but now you are in your golden years, or even if you aren't there yet, but you've somehow been left all alone, *keep reading.*

Blessings of the Woman

Genesis 49:25 is not a random blessing. It's Jacob speaking over Joseph. It is layered. "Blessings of heaven above…" "Blessings of the deep that lieth under…" "Blessings of the breasts…" "Blessings of the womb…" That's vertical and generational. Above. Below. Nurture. Fruitfulness. It's continuity language. It's covenant survival language.

This verse says that even if humans fail, the covenant stream does not dry up. Even if someone is discarded, the God of the father still helps. Even if seasons change, there are blessings stored above (divine provision) beneath (deep reserves unseen), in nurture (sustaining love), in legacy (fruitfulness that continues). It's a blessing that outlives betrayal.

Notice this: Jacob speaks this over Joseph, the son who was rejected by brothers, misunderstood, sold, forgotten, and imprisoned.

Drink waters out of thine own cistern, and running waters out of thine own well.

Let thy fountains be dispersed abroad, and rivers of waters in the streets.

Let them be only thine own, and not strangers' with thee.

Let thy fountain be blessed: and rejoice with the wife of thy youth.

Let her be as the loving hind and pleasant roe; let her breasts satisfy thee at all times; and be thou ravished always with her love. (Proverbs 5:15-19)

Joseph knows what abandonment feels like. And yet the blessing says God helped. God sustained. God blessed beyond the betrayal. That's not sentimental theology. That's historical resilience.

No one wants to be left alone – well not by a loved one, sometimes you may want a person to please go away. But under normal circumstances no one wants to be left, abandoned, discarded, dismissed, or erased. Genesis 49:25 whispers, *Even if you are, put away, discarded, or abandoned, God's covenant still operates above and beneath you.* That's not a tear. That's ballast.

The "I carried you for nine months" statement often is an appeal to obligation. It can be a reminder of sacrifice, a reminder of dependency, a reminder of origin, or an attempt to invoke guilt. In healthy form, it's gratitude language that means, "I labored for you. I nurtured you." In unhealthy form, it becomes leverage: "You owe me."

There's a difference between honoring motherhood and weaponizing it.

Genesis 49's "blessings of the breasts and of the womb" is covenantal language. It is provision, nurture, and generational continuity. It is not emotional leverage. It's about life given, not control over another's life.

In some traditional societies, including certain African cultures (and others globally), there are symbolic gestures involving motherhood and the body that function as severe rebuke or spiritual condemnation. These are usually ritualized acts meant to communicate any of the following:

- You have violated sacred maternal honor.
- You have broken filial duty.
- You have dishonored origin.

It is not about anatomy in a crude sense. It is about invoking the sacredness of the womb — the source of life — as moral authority.

Anthropologically, the womb is seen as covenantal territory. Sacred maternal authority can be honored. It can also be misused. When a mother appeals to the womb to bind an adult child indefinitely, that crosses from covenant honor into control. Motherhood grants honor. It does not grant ownership.

Carrying someone for nine months establishes origin. It does not establish permanent emotional indebtedness. Parental covenant is real, but it matures.

Marriage covenant is chosen, and binding. Manipulative attachment masquerading as covenant is something else entirely. Sacred things such as the womb, nurture life. They can either bless or be leveraged. It depends on if the soul of that person is aligned with God or not.

Life given does not equal life owned.

Genesis 49:25 — "blessings of the breasts and of the womb" — is not merely biological, it speaks of covenantal abundance. It means capacity to nourish, capacity to sustain, capacity to bring life, generational continuity, and provision that flows. It is not just about fertility; it is flourishing.

So, in that sense, the woman is **blessed**.

Being biologically capable does not automatically mean being spiritually aligned. But if she is spiritually aligned and prospered in her soul and you are married to her, that is in covenant with that womb and those breasts, should you walk away from that? *Can you?* Is it wise to do that?

If that is the womb and those are the breasts that you have covenanted with, whether since the days of your youth or not, but you decide to walk away, let's say to play the field and you do not want to covenant ever again, then you miss the blessing of the breasts and the womb because it is not about sex or having children. That covenanted woman is blessed to be a blessing. He who finds a wife finds a good thing and obtains favor from the Lord. If that is the good thing that you have found and obtained favor from the Lord because of it (Proverbs 18:22), should you just walk away?

All the *good things* that God created in Genesis; He blessed. Blessings are bestowed on those who are favored of the Lord. I am appealing to Wisdom to anyone who is reading this and is thinking about abandoning the wife of his youth.

How many stories have we heard about where a man left that wife and things didn't go well for him after that? There is a Biblical reason for that which I have just outlined. Pray for yourself and ask the Lord.

Conversely, a woman can have the physical blessing of the womb and yet be embittered, ungoverned in speech, evil, manipulative, wounded and speaking from that wound. Then what comes from her mouth may not be blessing. It may be the very opposite of a blessing.

Life and death are in the power of the tongue
(Proverbs 18:21)

You cannot give what you do not possess in alignment. A misaligned heart can weaponize even sacred authority. That doesn't negate the blessing. It means the blessing is being mishandled.

Think of Israel; covenanted, blessed, chosen, yet capable of uttering rebellion. The existence of blessing does not eliminate the possibility of corruption.

Motherhood carries honor. It carries sacred responsibility. It carries generational authority. But it is not immune from misuse. A mother speaking from fear can bind a child unnecessarily. A mother speaking from bitterness can reinforce dysfunction. A mother speaking from alignment can release life. A woman is specifically designed that whatever you give her, she multiplies. Will she multiply good things, or bad? This is about governance of the soul—both of yours.

A soul that is governed, blesses. A soul that is ungoverned, binds. Is the soul behind them is aligned with God? Do you know that soul? Are you treating that soul well?

Every harsh maternal or spousal word does not create a spiritual curse. Speech shapes atmosphere. Speech influences relationships. Speech can wound or build. Ultimate authority belongs to God, not to emotional utterance.

However, if a woman has been betrayed, left, or dealt treacherously with, there is real temptation toward bitterness that does not stay contained. That is the nature of bitterness; it leaks.

When children are present, words spoken in bitterness can shape how they view their father, how they view marriage, how they view loyalty, and also how they view themselves.

When she speaks life, stability grows. When she speaks from unhealed bitterness, instability spreads. The womb gives life; the mouth shapes it. If she has been wounded by the one who left her, then her pain is real. If she allows that pain to govern her speech, her children may inherit more than her story. They may inherit her injury. Is that transmission, curse, or is it both?

Her wound is not sin. Being betrayed was not her fault. But what she does with her wound matters.

The Lord restores my soul. (Psalm 23)

A ***Leaver*** answers for his treachery. A wounded woman must guard her mouth, so she does not multiply the damage.

The Tears of a Woman

God sees women's tears.

Hagar – Genesis 16 & 21 - Hagar weeps in the wilderness. God hears the voice of the child, and sees her affliction. She names Him: **El Roi — The God who sees me.** A discarded woman: seen by God. Always.

Hannah – 1 Samuel 1 - Hannah weeps bitterly. Eli mistakes her for drunk. But Scripture says: "She was in bitterness of soul, and prayed unto the Lord, and wept sore." God answers. Her tears were not weakness. They were petitions.

The Sinful Woman – Luke 7 - She weeps at Jesus' feet. Her tears become worship. Jesus defends her publicly. Her tears revealed repentance. His response revealed protection.

Mary (Lazarus) – John 11 says, She fell down at his feet… weeping.

And then, Jesus wept. He did not rebuke her tears. He entered them.

In the Gospels, **Luke 7:36–50**.

And stood at his feet behind him weeping, and began to wash his feet with tears, and did wipe them with the hairs of her head (Luke 7:38)

That woman is unnamed in Luke; she is described as “a sinner.” Her tears are not quiet. They are public. They are costly.

In Matthew 26, Mark 14, and John 12, a woman anoints Jesus with ointment from an alabaster box. In John 12, that woman is identified as Mary of Bethany. Luke’s weeping woman is not explicitly called Mary in the text. Tradition sometimes blends them, but Scripture does not clearly say they are the same person. Her tears were not weakness; They were worship. They were tears of release. They were also misunderstood.

The Pharisees judged her.

Jesus defended her.

Her tears were visible. Her devotion was costly. Her love was deep. But the room misread her.

A woman’s tears are not always manipulation. Sometimes they are reverence. Sometimes they are grief. Sometimes they are repentance. Sometimes they are love. Jesus did not shame her for them.

He said: “Her sins, which are many, are forgiven; for she loved much…” That’s recognition. She wept at His feet. He defended her honor.

Whether tears of anger, sadness, disappointment, loss or tears from a posture of determination or eyes toward the Lord in worship. *Who* would want to be the reason that woman is crying? ***Who***? *Why*? Is there not a cost for that? Is there no iniquity with hurting a fellow human being and most of all one that you were in covenant with – one you are supposed to protect, not to harm?

A woman who has been dealt treacherously with, abandoned, placed in a simulated covenant, making her think this was real or was going somewhere, but ultimately, betrayed, discarded, erased, or disrespected, will likely weep.

Tears are not evidence of weakness. They are evidence of value. You do not weep over what did not matter. Ultimately tears do not decide covenant; Time does. Tears do not determine justice; God does. Tears are honest, but they must not govern.

Who's To Blame?

I will take what you give in your strength and abandon you in your weakness. That is the unspoken mantra of a taker, a user, a *Leaver*.

Scripture says God notices. God remembers, and God intervenes. Amen.

Sometimes, however, people pray to invoke that intervention before the damage is complete. When abandonment is framed as something only the vulnerable person must pray against, the burden subtly shifts from the sinner to the potential victim.

That is *not* the Biblical pattern. Scripture does not primarily tell the widow, aging wife, or elderly mother to, *Pray harder so people don't abandon you.* Scripture primarily tells everyone else, "You will answer to God for how you treat the widow, the mature woman, children and other people in general—young or old.

Scripture assigns responsibility to the strong, not the weak. That is the nature of covenant; the stronger is in alliance with the weaker to benefit the weaker. Marriage is covenant. Biblically, accountability flows **upward**, not downward.

> Pure religion… is to care for orphans and widows in their distress. (James 1:27)

James does not say that widows must prevent abandonment, or aging women must remain "valuable enough," or that mothers must compete with youth. He places responsibility squarely on those with power, choice, and strength.

Abandonment is never framed as the older, weaker, or submitted person's failure. In some cases the one left has submitted all their relationship and perhaps he told he not to work and then suddenly leaves her. With what? With what means? How shall she live? Nowhere in Scripture do you see:

- "She aged incorrectly"
- "She lost beauty, so abandonment was understandable"
- "She prayed too little, so she was discarded"

Instead, Scripture names abandonment with words like *treachery, oppression, and injustice.*

God condemns the one who deals treacherously, not the one betrayed. In Malachi 2:16, trading in a spouse for a "newer model" is explicitly framed as moral failure in the Bible. God allows divorce, but everything legal is not expedient.

Jesus reinforces loyalty when culture permits disposal. First-century culture already allowed men to dismiss wives, older women to become invisible, and widows to be neglected. Jesus does not accommodate that culture.

What God has joined together, let no one separate. (Matthew 19:6)

That statement protects the one with less leverage, not the one with more. That is what covenant is about.

Children are not exempt, and adult children are morally bound. This is often softened today, but Scripture is blunt.

If a widow has children or grandchildren, they should learn first to put their religion into practice by caring for their own family. (1 Timothy 5:4)

Neglecting aging parents is treated as faith failure, not lifestyle choice. And it applies to sons and daughters, biological and adopted children, whether at proximity or at a distance.

This is not about women up in arms or praying that this doesn't happen to them. This behavior or outcome applies to all people, all of society, universally. It's not women, pray this doesn't happen to you" --, No, it's, "People, do not do this; it is dangerous because it unintentionally excuses abandonment. It spiritualizes betrayal. It individualizes what Scripture treats as communal sin. It can even imply, If it happens, the victim of that meanness *missed something*.

That is not Biblical justice. That is spiritual gaslighting.

The Biblical prayer is not "prevent me from being abandoned." The *correct* prayer emphasis is twofold. For the vulnerable the prayer is for protection, provision, dignity, companionship, and justice. As well it is for sustenance in God, right relationship and to age well, with Grace.

For everyone else there should be conviction, restraint, remembrance and appreciation of what the previous generation has done for you. There should be covenantal fear; God hates broken and disrespected covenant. There should be moral clarity.

The psalmist condemns those who "kill the widow… and say, 'The Lord does not see.'" *Psalm* 94:6–7

God's response throughout Scripture is essentially, "I see. And I will answer."

Dealt Treacherously With

There is a particular kind of injury that does not leave bruises; it leaves bewilderment. It is when a woman (especially, but this can apply to men as well) is dealt with in a treacherous way.

A woman does not have to be old to be abandoned. She does not have to be mature to be used. She does not have to have lived decades to be handled carelessly. Some women learn early what it means to be dealt treacherously with.

There is the man who enters like a student of your interior world. He studies you. He asks questions. He observes what makes you laugh. What makes you soften. What wounds you carry. What you value. What you fear. He appears attentive. He appears present. But he is not learning you in order to cherish you.

You don't know that. You like the attention, maybe even need it. You are young or immature. He is polished, maybe charming. He may be charmed with an anointing that is not from God.

Like a human *monitoring spirit*, he is mapping you. Once he believes he understands what makes you tick, once he believes he has extracted what he came for, he disappears.

There is no confrontation. You two usually have no covenant. There is no explanation. Poof! He's gone. You are left with the unsettling realization that someone was present with you, but not **<u>for</u>** you. That is treachery.

Ghosted.

On deliverance ground they say the assignment is over. He got or did what he came for. Chances are very good it wasn't just money or sex. It was more, spiritually speaking, and you may not know what that assignment was until weeks, months, or years later when you finally realize you are missing something spiritually that you usually have, but oddly, no longer have. Oh, I don't know, like—favor? Where did it go? Mr. Soave took it whenever he took it, however he took it, when you laid it down. They say when you have sex with a guy, whether your covenant spouse or not, you are baring not just your body, but your whole soul and that dreamy person may be there to take it.

Kudos to you if you peeped his game, if you discerned it and didn't compromise in any way. When that one suddenly leaves it is because of Failed Assignment.

There are too many forms of treachery. There is another type of person who lingers, attaches and slowly disassembles your life. Not always with cruelty that can be quoted, but with calculated erosion. He questions your clarity. He questions your memory. He questions your instincts. He questions your standards, your observations and your conclusions. He makes you question yourself, until what once stood upright begins to bend.

Some men do not enter a woman's life to build with her. They enter to see if they can access her. Access to her body, resources, admiration, emotions, mind, and or labor. Once access is secured and consumed, the urgency fades. The extraction is complete. The woman is left asking, "What did I do wrong?"

Nothing.

You think he is learning how to love you. He is learning how to reach you. Once you have confided and he has confined you, he confirms that he can--, and something changes. The warmth cools. The pursuit relaxes. The energy shifts.

Then eventually, or suddenly, he is gone.

Little by little, the woman who stood upright begins to lean. She is not weak—well, she never used to be. She is being worn down. Some people do not destroy loudly. They erode quietly. Erosion is harder to prove.

If you have ever thought: "I feel different than I used to feel." If you have ever felt smaller in someone's presence. If you have ever replayed conversations trying to understand how you became the so-called "unreasonable one" If you have ever watched someone pull away the moment you needed steadiness. Then you have tasted treachery. Not drama. Not imagination. Treachery.

The young woman reading this may think, "That happens to foolish girls."

Well, not just ---,

It also happens to generous women, to beautiful women, to intelligent women, even to successful women. It happens to women who believe words. It happens to women who assume that interest equals intention.

So, he left and it was not because you failed. Because he finished. Still, it left you abandoned, or feeling so.

Oh no, it's not because you were weak. It is because someone learned which screws to loosen, which buttons to push. Sad, but some people do not love women; they audit them. They assess them for capacity. They compete with them and you don't have any idea they are competing because you don't think like that. Really, why would you? They test elasticity. They evaluate emotional yield, then they try to lessen a person, break them down, use them up, and then they move on.

This is not romance gone wrong. This is extraction. Scripture has a word for it: Treacherous. To deal treacherously is to violate trust without declaring war. It is betrayal without spectacle.

None of this stuff only happens to older women. It happens to young women who are bright, hopeful, trusting, faithful, and open. They are just out here living their lives and are still generous with their inner world.

Ecclesiastes reminds us that life moves quickly. The young woman reading this will one day be the woman on the cover. Time does not wait. Patterns do not wait. Recognition must come early. The earlier the better, but not to become jaded, but to walk aware and be wise. The difference between her now and that woman is not innocence. It is accumulation. Recognition. Experience. She will know the patterns by then. But she does not have to learn them the hard way.

There are men who enter relationships seeking covenant and there are men who enter relationships seeking advantage. The one seeking covenant builds. The one seeking advantage studies. The one seeking covenant protects. The one seeking advantage probes. The one seeking covenant stays. The one seeking advantage vanishes.

The woman who has experienced the latter must not internalize the treachery as her deficiency.

Being studied is not the same as being known. Being used is not the same as being chosen. Being dismantled is not the same as being refined.

A woman who has been dealt treacherously with does not need revenge. She needs recognition. She needs language. She needs to understand that what happened to her has a name. It's not drama, exaggeration, or overreaction. It's Treachery.

Once named, it loses some of its power.

The God who says, **"I will never leave you nor forsake you,"** also says He hates treachery. He sees it. He weighs it. He does not confuse extraction with love. He does not call erosion intimacy. He does not reward opportunism with covenant. So, if you were dealt treacherously with in youth, you were not foolish. You were generous, open, and trusting. Trust misplaced does not make you unworthy, but it does make someone else accountable.

God is watching, and He is not at the distance that many think He is.

The mature woman on the cover was young once. She knows what it means to be studied. She knows what it means to be left. She knows what it means to rebuild. She is still standing.

Because of the God she serves, Jehovah Roi she is not and never will be forsaken or forgotten.

This Is Why He Must Love Your Soul

Biblically men are told to love their wives. Women are not commanded such; they are told to honor and respect their husbands.

He must love your soul. Not your usefulness. Not your youth. Not your beauty. Not your availability. Not your admiration. Not your resilience. Not your bank account, paycheck or your 401K.

Your soul.

Why? Because anything less will not hold. If he loves your beauty, time will test it. If he loves your body, age will test it. If he loves your strength, fatigue will test it. If he loves your compliance, growth will threaten it. But if he loves your soul— He will not panic when outward appearance changes. He will not retreat when you mature. Is he so farsighted that he can't see that he is also changing? Don't you still love *him*?

In every relationship, several days a month a man is tested. There are ordinary days when love is easy. And there are days when it is not. There are days when she is strong and radiant. And there are days when she is tired, in pain, or unsettled. Who is *he* on those days?

Is he patient when she is not sparkling? Is he gentle when she is not easy? Is he steady when she is inconvenient? How is he when she is not pouring out to him? When she is not ministering to him?

Not only that, if they do marry then there will be a 40-week time period at least once as they gestate and prepare to birth a child and she will probably be different that whole time. Good or bad. Who is *he* then? Good or bad?

The right one will not punish you for *being*. He will not punish you for being a woman or for being yourself if he is a governed soul with proper motives.

He will not punish you for thinking. He will not disappear when you require depth. A man who loves your soul is not studying you to master you. He is standing before you to honor you. He does not need access. He seeks covenant. He does not extract. He invests. He does not erode. He builds.

(Of course, this works both ways. This book is not about how to be worshipped and adored by your spouse.)

Now, back to the book: If he does not love your soul, he will eventually consume those surface or temporal things that he admires. When the surface offering is spent, so is he. This is why he must love your soul. Not your shine. Not your service. Not your softness, but your soul. He must love your soul.

The stored-up treasures of the flesh and affects of the natural life can all rust or rot or be stolen, but as long as you possess your soul and prosper it, it will not depreciate, wrinkle, or wilt.

The man who loves your soul will not either.

Abandonment is never the fault of the person who aged. It is the moral failure of the person who left.

Instead of "Let me pray this doesn't happen to me," this book declares that:

- Life happens to everyone.
- **Even if people fail, God does not.**
- **Those who abandon will answer for it.**

That's not fear-based, it is covenant-based.

For you who are steadfast, Scripture agrees with you and is on your side.

What Drove a Man to This?

Why a man would do this is not really the question as much as he did it. We can look at it not merely to cast blame but to understand, and to govern ourselves accordingly. It may not even be to reason with that man because he may be resolved, resigned, or past reason by this time.

If it is that you work and have money or give him money and now you've stopped, that's obvious. If it was that you cooked and cleaned and served him and now you can't or won't, then you were hired help, whether you got paid or not. If you are no longer serving his purposes, and he is a user, then you have got to go.

If he is an owned man tied down by looks, appearance and what the world thinks of him and his arm candy and you're the candy, but you don't look delicious anymore, well that should tell you everything.

It may not all be his fault. A woman can tear down her own house and drive a man away, but when he is captive, he is merely led away. He lets the temptation lead him. Temptation for what? New experience. Beauty, success, fame, money… whatever his temptation is.

Catering to a shallow man will never make him deep. Challenging a shallow man, may or it may not. A prideful man will either shut his challenger down, or run off.

If it is that you raised y'all's kids and now they are gone, that's another thing, the ultimate in disrespect.

If it is a strange woman, then we know immediately that man is weak and not in full possession of himself. There are billions of women in the world, will every one of them tempt him? None should if he is married, that is why I question his spiritual and moral strength.

Spiritual Integrity

A man needs to have possession of his own soul. A man needs to not be owned. A man needs to be in authority and set under authority. Yes, for himself first and then if he is taking on a wife and potentially or planning to have a family he has to exercise authority over the marriage, the home, the spouse, the kids. Authority means oversight and protection, not ownership and lordship.

If he is weak and only *performing* authority over his marriage and home, the whole thing is easy pickings for outside influences. If he is not operating in spiritual integrity and authority under God, then lesser powers can take over what he has. On deliverance ground, many men are simply led away. They leave their wife, home, family, and children to go and be with a strange woman, and they don't even know why. Why is because they were spiritually weak, distracted, foolish, tempted and temptable and to the ones he deceived, it makes him contemptible. Witchcraft can do this, therefore a man has to be spiritually strong to get, have, and maintain his marriage and family. Let no man say when he is tempted, that he is tempted of God (James 1:13).

Said plainly, that man can be bewitched.

It is possible for a man to be so influenced or *bewitched*, that he abruptly leaves his family. Spiritual weakness and lack of integrity can leave a man vulnerable to temptations or influences that draw him away from his responsibilities and loved ones. Some kinds of witchcraft specialize in this. When a man is not grounded in spiritual authority or is distracted and tempted, he may act against his character and commitments, sometimes without fully understanding why he is compelled to go. This is not merely a matter of external seduction but also of inner spiritual condition, showing how being led astray is often a sign of deeper issues within.

The man that is driven away can be manipulated spiritually and when he does nothing about it (spiritually) he may begin to think these are his own ideas, or he may think that his dreams, if they are being manipulated for instance, are true. For example, *spirit spouse's* goal is to separate marriages. Dream manipulation to that end can be anything from threat, to accusing the natural spouse of infidelity or something as heinous, all the way to convincing a man that his sexuality is the opposite of what it actually is. He may never tell anyone, do nothing about these dream attacks, and they are attacks. Next thing you know--, he's gone. Either off, away, hidden or to live some life that is the antithesis of his real life.

Had that man been spiritually protected – not by a pastor, but in Christ himself, for himself, along with whatever else he needed, he would have been strong enough to withstand the test and win the battle. *What will he tell God?*

Such abandonment is not simply a result of personal desire but can be the outcome of failing to possess one's own soul and succumbing to lesser spiritual influences, even occult, in the night, in the dream. Those are the forces that take over when spiritual integrity falters.

This has been seen over the years as the man who went to the store and never came back. The man who may have even faked his own death to move onto another place and another life. The man who was gone for months or years and then just came back as if he just took control of his senses again.

How can I say that? No wife was involved but didn't the Prodigal Son just leave, party and then got desperate and just came back home. Doesn't certain demonic charge, oppression and possession affect the minds of people, and they do as they are told. Aren't people 'brainwashed' who join cults and the like? How is that done? With words that have spiritual charge and that anointing on those words is from the dark kingdom, not God. Didn't Nebuchadnezzar think he was livestock for seven years, but then came back to his senses?

Don't people describe people who act out of character as, 'they took leave of their senses'? Didn't legion, over in the Gadarenes get his deliverance and when he was next seen he was "in his right mind"?

Replacement Culture: Trading People for Seasons

Replacement culture does not announce itself as cruelty. It presents as progress. It speaks in the language of "growth," "alignment," "deserving happiness," and "living your best life." It borrows the vocabulary of freedom while quietly redefining loyalty as optional and people as interchangeable.

In replacement culture, nothing is meant to last longer than its peak usefulness. Phones are replaced when they slow. Cars are replaced when repairs cost more than novelty. Jobs are replaced when productivity dips.

Sadly, though rarely admitted, people are replaced when they age.

This culture did not begin with women, but women feel it first and longest. Mothers who gave decades to caregiving. Wives who invested their youth, fertility, emotions and labor, and unpaid support. Women whose strength was spent in service rather than self-preservation.

Replacement culture does not call this abandonment. It calls it *moving on*. Scripture calls it something else entirely.

There is a lie beneath the language. Replacement culture rests on a single, corrosive assumption: *Worth is tied to what someone can currently provide.* When provision shifts from beauty to wrinkles, from earning to needing, from caregiving to dependence— worth is quietly reassessed.

This logic is never applied equally.

A man's aging is often reframed as gravitas, experience, or authority. A woman's aging is framed as loss. Scripture does not share this bias. From beginning to end, the Bible treats time as something that *reveals* value, not erodes it.

The modern world fears aging because it exposes motives. Covenant does not.

Wisdom comes with age and Wisdom is an upgrade, not a downgrade.

Covenant was designed for seasons, not peaks. Covenant is not a promise to stay *while it feels good*. It is a promise to stay *when it does not*. That is why covenant language appears alongside words like faithfulness, endurance, remembrance, and witness. These are not words of convenience; they are words of time.

From Genesis onward, covenant is never framed as conditional on performance remaining high. God binds

Himself to people knowing they will fail, weaken, age, and disappoint. That is Divine commitment.

When humans adopt replacement logic, they are not being modern, they are being **anti-covenantal**.

Aging exposes character because youth and beauty can hide many sins. Strength can mask selfishness. Beauty can delay betrayal. Success can excuse neglect. But aging removes leverage. When someone no longer has youth to trade, strength to offer, or admiration to generate, the question becomes unavoidable:

Were they loved for who they were—or for what they provided?

Replacement culture answers this question brutally. Scripture answers it justly.

When Scripture speaks of *"the wife of your youth,"* it is not romanticizing the past. It is naming a moral obligation that survives the passage of time, especially since a vow was made. Malachi uses language that is startlingly blunt: abandonment of a long-standing spouse is called **treachery**. This is not incompatibility, growth or transition. It is pure and simple: Treachery. That word exists because something sacred was violated.

Replacement culture despises that word because it refuses to flatter desire.

Being "Phased Out" is violence against a person, no matter how it is phrased. Abandonment does not always arrive with dramatic exits. Often it arrives as emotional withdrawal, financial neglect, reduced presence, silent replacement. People are not always thrown away. Sometimes they are simply **moved aside**. Scripture notices this too. The Bible repeatedly condemns those who: consume devotion and then disappear. Nobody who benefits from sacrifice and then detaches is beneath God's radar. Thos who grow strong on someone else's labor and leave them weakened--, God sees it all. God does not miss sins—large, small, hidden, quiet, loud. It doesn't matter; He doesn't miss them.

Women are often the first casualties. This is not ideology, but it is reality. Women often pause careers for family earn less across a lifetime. They live longer, outlast spouses, and shoulder unpaid labor. Replacement culture punishes these sacrifices retroactively.

Scripture honors them.

This is why God identifies Himself repeatedly as defender of widows—not because they are weak, but because others pretend not to see them. To be unseen by users and ***Leavers*** is not accidental; it is convenient.

Replacement Culture tells us people are seasonal. It refuses to admit that loyalty might limit desire. It is true, though not often admitted that covenant might restrain impulse. Responsibility might survive attraction if it is allowed. So, this culture instead reframes departure as inevitability and abandonment as evolution. Scripture refuses this reframing. It insists that character is revealed not in who we pursue—but in who we refuse to abandon.

This book will not ask how to age more attractively, or how to remain indispensable. It will not show how to pray betrayal away. It will ask harder questions such as: *Who benefits from replacement logic? Who bears its cost? What does God say to those who justify leaving the vulnerable behind?*

Covenant says otherwise. The God in my Bible does not side with what is fashionable. He sides with what is faithful.

There is another thing about life and experiences and even run ins with other people – when God created man He crowned us with glory and honor. By running up on life and takers for a long time, a person's glory can be stolen, eroded; their star may be stolen, so others may not see the value in a person who appears to have little or no glory remaining. This is speaking more about that person than the aged woman. It is telling that the person was looking for that person's glory and like a vine stripped by locusts, someone or some others got to it first. So, they keep it moving. Another reason a mature woman may be left is that she is wise, she is not foolish and that can be too much work for the unserious male or the opportunist.

If the worth of any person is assessed to be only what she can do for you; then you should keep stepping because the preciousness of what God created will not be discounted. If the woman has been known or allegedly known for years by the man who leaves, then perhaps he really never knew her and never valued her as a human being. God will deal with this.

Covenant Is Not Seasonal

Covenant is one of the most misused words in modern religious language—and one of the least understood.

In contemporary speech, covenant is often treated as a poetic synonym for commitment, sincerity, or intensity of feeling. But in Scripture, covenant is not emotional language at all. It is legal, moral, and binding. It is not measured by desire. It is measured by endurance. A covenant is not made for the best season of life. It is made because seasons change.

If human beings remained strong, attractive, productive, agreeable, and healthy throughout life, covenants would be unnecessary. Affection alone would suffice. Mutual benefit would keep everyone faithful.

But Scripture assumes the opposite. From the opening pages of Genesis, covenant is introduced into a world where bodies fail, strength fades, people disappoint, time takes its toll. Covenant is God's answer to instability—not a romantic ideal layered on top of it. That is why covenant language is consistently paired with words like: *forever, remember, witness, faithful, steadfast.* These are not words for moments; they are words for **Time**.

Seasonal thinking is anti-covenantal. Replacement culture trains people to think seasonally: "This was good *for a time*." "We've grown apart." "That chapter has ended." These phrases sound mature and measured, but Scripture evaluates them differently when they are used to justify abandonment.

Seasonal thinking assumes *When conditions change, obligations expire.* Covenant directly contradicts that assumption. Covenant says *When conditions change, faithfulness is tested.*

Time does not weaken covenant. Time reveals whether covenant was ever truly honored.

God does not covenant with the ideal version of people. One of the most overlooked truths in Scripture is this: God never covenants with people at their peak. He covenants knowing exactly who they will become. God binds Himself to Abraham before age and weakness reshape his body. He binds Himself to Israel knowing they will wander, complain, and fail. He binds Himself to humanity knowing decline, death, and limitation are unavoidable.

This is not Divine oversight; it is Divine intent. Covenant is God's declaration that worth does not expire when usefulness changes. When humans abandon covenants because seasons shift, they are not being honest—they are being selective.

Regarding, *the wife of your youth,* Malachi does not invoke youth to stir nostalgia. It invokes youth to establish continuity of responsibility. The implication is unmistakable: *If covenant was formed when she was young, it remains binding when she is now older.*

Time does not dissolve obligation. Time confirms it. This is why Scripture uses the word *treachery* for abandonment. Treachery is not the breaking of a casual agreement—it is the violation of a sworn bond. Seasonal logic cannot coexist with covenant logic.

Endurance is not a flaw in love. Modern culture often portrays endurance as weakness: staying too long, settling, refusing growth. Scripture portrays endurance as proof. Love that only survives pleasure is not love—it is alignment of interests. Love that survives inconvenience, decline, and loss is covenantal.

This does not mean endurance excuses abuse or injustice. Scripture never sanctifies harm. But it does make a sharp distinction between suffering that results from betrayal and difficulty that comes from remaining faithful.

The first is condemned. The second is honored.

Aging is central to covenant theology. Aging is not a side issue in Scripture; it is central. Aging removes leverage, exposes motives, strips illusions, clarifies loyalty. This is why Scripture repeatedly elevates: gray hair, long faithfulness, perseverance over time

Covenant is not designed to keep people young. It is designed to keep people faithful. Any theology that subtly treats aging as a liability has already departed from covenant thinking.

God's got a long memory whereas humans are prone to forget. To forget in Scripture is not merely to fail to recall. It is to withdraw recognition and care. Human beings forget when someone no longer benefits them, when someone slows them down, or someone reminds them of time passing. God explicitly defines Himself as One who does not do this.

When Scripture says God *remembers*, it means He continues to act on behalf of someone—even when others have moved on. Covenant is sustained not by emotion, but by memory with responsibility attached.

What breaks covenant is not time; it is desire without restraint. Covenant does not fail because people age. It fails because desire is elevated above duty. Replacement culture trains people to believe that desire is self-validating. Scripture insists desire must be governed.

Covenant places boundaries on impulse precisely because impulse changes. Without covenant, the strongest always win—and the weakest are always left behind.

If covenant is seasonal, then loyalty is meaningless. If loyalty is optional, then faith is performative. If faith is performative, then Scripture's moral framework collapses.

This is why abandonment is never treated lightly in the Bible. It is not simply relational failure—it is covenantal violation. Covenant violations, rupture, and breakage--, they always matter to God.

This book does not argue that people must feel the same forever. Scripture never demands frozen emotion, but it does demand this: Obligation outlives attraction. Responsibility outlasts desire. Covenant survives seasons. Anything less is not maturity; it is betrayal with better language.

Treachery: The Word Scripture Uses on Purpose

Scripture is careful with language. When it chooses a word, it does so deliberately—especially when naming sin.

That is why the Bible does not describe abandonment with soft terms. It does not call it *drift*, *misalignment*, *self-discovery*, or *closure*. When covenant is violated, Scripture reaches for a word with weight:

Treachery.

Scripture refuses euphemisms. Modern culture survives on euphemism. Harmful actions are rebranded to reduce moral friction. Betrayal becomes growth. Neglect becomes "boundaries. Abandonment becomes choosing myself.

Scripture does not cooperate with this project.

When language is softened, conscience is dulled. When sin is renamed, accountability dissolves. The Bible resists this by calling things what they are—especially when the vulnerable pay the price.

Treachery is a word reserved for **violations of trust where obligation already existed**.

You cannot betray a stranger. You can only betray someone to whom you owed loyalty.

Treachery is not the failure of feeling. It is the failure of faithfulness. It is not momentary weakness. It is sustained disloyalty. It is not mutual drifting. It is one party breaking a bond while continuing to benefit from the break.

This is why Scripture uses the word sparingly—and pointedly.

In Malachi, God speaks directly to men who have abandoned long-standing wives. He does not analyze their emotional journeys. He does not validate their dissatisfaction. He names their action for what it is: **treachery.**

The offense is not aging. The offense is abandonment after covenant.

Why *no one is perfect* does not apply here. Scripture is generous toward human weakness. It is not indulgent toward covenant betrayal. Many sins are treated with patience, instruction, and restoration. Treachery is treated with severity because it **destroys trust structures**—families, households, and communities.

This is why Scripture does not excuse abandonment with terms such as unmet expectations, boredom, changing preferences, personal fulfillment narratives. None of these nullify obligation.

Covenant was never based on emotional permanence. It was based on moral responsibility.

The difference between failure and betrayal is that failure acknowledges obligation and falls short. Betrayal denies obligation altogether.

Scripture differentiates between the two.

A person who struggles within covenant but remains accountable is treated differently from a person who discards covenant to pursue desire. One is met with Mercy. The other is confronted with judgment.

Replacement culture collapses it.

Treachery often targets the aging. Treachery frequently appears at life's inflection points: when beauty fades, when illness arrives, when earning capacity drops, when caregiving reverses direction. These moments reveal whether covenant was ever honored, or merely tolerated. Aging does not create treachery. It reveals it. There is no way the lessening of strength in a covenant partner would create treachery in a person. It was always there. It may have been seen before when his oxen wouldn't pull, his horse wouldn't gallop, or his dog wouldn't fetch. Pay attention to how people treat others and animals.

Scripture is unflinching here because the harm is predictable. When someone is abandoned at their most vulnerable, the damage multiplies economic instability, emotional devastation, loss of community standing, and spiritual disorientation.

God does not treat this as unfortunate; He treats it as unjust.

Silence can enable treachery. One of the reasons treachery thrives is silence. Families avoid confrontation. Communities look away. Churches stay neutral. Neutrality in the face of treachery is not Mercy; it is permission. Treacherous people don't understand Grace. To them Grace is permission or what they did was so clever that they got away with it.

Scripture never models this kind of restraint. Prophets speak precisely because silence would protect the wrong party. The Bible is not embarrassed to take sides when covenant is violated. It consistently sides with the one who was wronged. People change is not a moral defense. Scripture assumes people change. The one who is judging the one that changed, have themselves also changed. That is the point of covenant. Change does not dissolve obligation; it tests it. To argue that growth requires abandonment is to redefine growth as selfishness with spiritual vocabulary attached. Scripture rejects this outright.

Growth that requires betrayal is not maturity. It is appetite with justification.

God's language is a warning, not an overreaction. When Scripture calls abandonment treachery, it is not exaggerating to provoke guilt. It is issuing a warning.

Treachery is corrosive. It teaches the strong that desire outranks duty. It teaches the vulnerable that loyalty is unsafe. Unchecked, it becomes generational.

This is why God intervenes so strongly on behalf of those who are abandoned. He understands what treachery does long after the betrayer has "moved on."

Many people who would never identify as cruel participate in treachery simply by rationalizing, justifying and adopting softer language. They tell themselves things like, "I didn't promise forever." "I have to live my truth." "This is just how life works."

Scripture dismantles these defenses with one word: **Treachery.** That is not because God lacks compassion—but because He values covenant.

This book does not claim that relationships are easy. It does not deny that seasons are difficult. It does not pretend covenant requires no sacrifice.

NOT FORSAKEN OR FORGOTTEN does insist on this: **When someone benefits from years of loyalty and then abandons that person in weakness, Scripture does not call it personal growth, it calls it treachery.** And God does not ignore it.

The Myth of the Aging Woman's Failure

In the natural, blame can shift to the vulnerable, but Scripture never supports that shift. There is a quiet accusation that follows many women into later seasons of life. It is rarely spoken aloud, but it is often implied: *She did something wrong.* She did not age well enough. She did not remain attractive enough. She did not adapt fast enough. She did not hold attention the way she once did.

This accusation is not Biblical. It is cultural and devastating.

Blame, too often gets reassigned. Replacement culture does not like to admit betrayal. It prefers explanations that protect the one who leaves. So, responsibility is subtly reassigned.

The story shifts from, *Someone broke covenant, She failed to keep herself desirable.* It depends on the heart and the guilt of the person telling the story. This shift is powerful because it sounds reasonable. It reframes abandonment as inevitability and betrayal as consequence. There was a young married couple who worked the same hours at the same business. They carpooled to and from work together, a 30-minute commute each way, at least. The husband became angry more than once a week when there was no hot meal at home when he got there. Like how? There were both at the same place all day, together, though in different departments. This was his beginning excuse to show her and others that she was faulty, and to set up his leaving, which he did a few years after they were married.

Scripture does not permit this reframing. Nowhere in the Bible is a woman blamed for being abandoned because she aged, weakened, gave birth, or changed. The absence of that logic in Scripture is not accidental. It is corrective.

Aging is not moral failure. Aging is not a lapse in discipline. It is not spiritual negligence. It is not evidence of diminished worth. Scripture treats aging as honor-bearing, not shame-bearing.

Gray hair is associated with Wisdom. Long life is spoken of as blessing. Endurance is praised, not pitied. The idea that aging women become less deserving of loyalty is entirely foreign to Biblical thought. That idea comes from economies—not covenants.

Women carry this lie more heavily. Women are often judged by visibility, appearance, fertility, energy, and or adaptability. When these shift, the culture implies something has been lost.

Scripture never defines women by these measures.

Instead, Scripture highlights faithfulness, sacrifice, endurance, unseen labor. These qualities do not peak in youth. They deepen with time. The problem is not that women age. The problem is that culture worships novelty.

Even well-meaning spiritual language can reinforce this myth. Phrases like: "Stay prayed up," "Remain desirable," "Guard your marriage by keeping yourself," may sound practical, but they carry an unspoken implication: *If abandonment happens, you failed to prevent it.*

Scripture never places this burden on the vulnerable. It places moral responsibility on the one who chooses to leave.

When covenant is broken, Scripture does not examine the aging body of the one left behind. It examines the heart of the one who departed. In Malachi, the charge is not that the woman changed. The charge is that the man acted treacherously.

Scripture does not say *She was no longer pleasing.*

It says to the one who was unfaithful: *You were unfaithful.*

When women internalize the myth of personal failure, the damage multiplies. They tolerate neglect longer than they should, excuse betrayal, minimize their own pain, and accept isolation as deserved. This is not humility. It is harm.

Scripture never asks the wounded to explain away injustice.

This myth persists even in faith communities. Churches often avoid confronting abandonment because it complicates pastoral care. It is easier to offer individual coping strategies than communal accountability. So, the message becomes: "Heal yourself. Pray harder. Improve yourself" while those who do the abandoning (I call them **Leavers**) are rarely challenged. This is not neutrality. It is imbalance. And imbalance always favors power.

God's attention is not on her aging—it is on his leaving. Throughout Scripture, God's gaze consistently moves toward the one who was wronged. He sees the woman pushed aside, the mother forgotten, the widow ignored. He identifies Himself as their defender—not because they are flawless, but because they were faithful.

God does not ask the ones left what they did to deserve abandonment. He asks the abandoner why covenant was violated.

This book rejects the lie that aging women are responsible for being left. Not because women are perfect. But because Scripture is clear. Aging is not betrayal. Needing care is not failure. Losing cultural leverage is not sin.

Abandonment is.

Dear Reader: The vulnerable are not on trial. Time does not cancel worth. Value doesn't leak out of a person; if anything, they should get more valuable in the eyes of those who are in covenant with them or those who say they love them. Covenant does not require self-erasure to survive. Blame belongs where Scripture places it, not where a man who is avoiding responsibility is trying to place it.

Let the clarity in this chapter be the beginning of justice.

Husbands: Covenant Does Not Expire

Scripture addresses men directly when abandonment enters marriage. Had God seen a pattern?

Scripture does not speak vaguely to husbands. When covenant failure enters a marriage, the Bible addresses men directly, clearly, and without euphemism. This is not because men are uniquely flawed. It is because Scripture recognizes where power and leverage most often sit and holds responsibility there.

Covenant does not expire when desire changes. It does not thin with time. It does not renegotiate itself around comfort. If it did, it would not be covenant at all.

Scripture speaks to husbands without ambiguity. Throughout the Bible, when abandonment occurs within marriage, God does not ask husbands how they felt about it first. He asks what they did with what they were entrusted. Some were entrusted with a wife. What did that man do with that wife?

Marriage is treated as stewardship before it is treated as companionship. A husband is not merely someone who feels affection. He is someone who has sworn responsibility. This is why Scripture does not frame marital faithfulness as a mood, but as a charge.

The wife of your youth is a legal phrase. When God speaks through Malachi about *"the wife of your youth,"* He is not invoking sentimentality. He is invoking continuity of obligation. The meaning is stark: The woman you covenanted with when she was young is the same woman you are bound to when she is not.

Youth establishes history. Time establishes proof. Abandonment after years of **benefit** is not framed as incompatibility. It is framed as **treachery** because the bond was never conditional on youth remaining intact. Didn't both of them age?

Desire is not authority. One of the most dangerous cultural lies is that desire grants permission. Scripture never treats desire as self-validating. It treats desire as something that must be governed. Attraction is acknowledged. Impulse is restrained. Responsibility to govern oneself accordingly remains.

This is why Jesus' words in Matthew are so disruptive: "What God has joined together, let no one separate." That statement is not romantic; it is legal, it is protective. It places a boundary around the covenant precisely because desire fluctuates.

Midlife is a test, not an excuse. Many abandonments occur not in early failure, but in midlife transition—when aging becomes visible and novelty becomes tempting.

Scripture does not treat this as mysterious. Midlife exposes whether covenant was anchored in commitment or convenience. When a husband abandons a wife after years of shared labor, caregiving, sacrifice, and support, Scripture does not describe him as *rediscovering himself.* It describes him as breaking faith.

Provision is not optional faithfulness. Biblically, provision is not merely financial. It includes presence, protection advocacy, constancy. A husband who withdraws emotionally, financially, or relationally while remaining legally attached is not excused. Silent abandonment is still abandonment. Scripture does not allow men to redefine faithfulness downward as long as paperwork remains intact. Covenant is lived, not filed.

The sentence, *I'm not happy,* is not a moral defense. Scripture never condemns honesty about struggle. It does condemn the use of dissatisfaction as justification for betrayal. Happiness is not the measure of righteousness. Faithfulness is.

A husband may struggle. He may grieve. He may require counsel. What he may not do, Biblically speaking, is use personal discontent as license to discard covenant.

The cost of male abandonment is not private. When husbands abandon covenant, the consequences ripple outward. Wives lose security, families fracture, communities destabilize, and children inherit confusion.

This is why Scripture treats marital treachery as a public moral issue, not a private lifestyle choice. God does not pretend abandonment only affects the two people involved. He names its generational weight.

God's Judgment is not gendered, but responsibility is specific. This chapter is not an indictment of men as a class. It is an insistence that those entrusted with authority must answer for how they used it. Scripture does not spare husbands because leadership is difficult. It holds them accountable *because* leadership carries weight.

To abandon covenant is to misuse authority.

This book does not deny that marriages can fail. It does not deny complexity or hardship. But it insists on this truth: Covenant does not end when attraction fades. If it did, where would anyone **half past cute** be with God? Responsibility does not dissolve when desire shifts. And a husband does not become righteous by redefining betrayal as growth. God is not confused by better language.

Husbands are addressed directly in Scripture regarding abandonment. Desire is not permission. Provision includes presence and protection. Covenant survives seasons of dissatisfaction.

Faithfulness is not proven in youth.
It is proven over time.

God Sees

A wife of youth. The woman who gave her best years, believed the vow, trusted the covenant, and found herself dismissed. Isaiah does something powerful He uses feminine imagery to describe covenant breach.

There are tears that come from weakness. And there are tears that come from violation.

Isaiah speaks of a woman forsaken. A wife of youth. Refused. He does not mock her tears. He does not minimize her grief. A man with a selfish agenda might, but God will not tell a woman she imagined it.

God names it: Forsaken. Grieved in spirit. Refused—, that is where many women live quietly.

A woman's tears are not manipulation. They are release. But after tears must come alignment. Because a woman may cry for what she lost, but she must not beg for what God did not join.

God records real tears. They are not wasted. They are not theatrical. They are not forgotten.

For the Lord hath called thee as a woman forsaken and grieved in spirit, and a wife of youth, when thou wast refused, saith thy God. (Isaiah 54:6–8)

God compares Israel to a woman forsaken. a wife of youth, grieved in spirit. And then He says,

For a small moment have I forsaken thee; but with great mercies will I gather thee.

This verse is about covenant restoration. It is about a woman who felt rejected. God speaks tenderness — not condemnation. Lord, let the ***Leaver*** know that no matter how he sets the narrative or tries to belittle her or run her down, God sees and He is not so far away that He can't see straight. God knows. He knows all. He knows who did what.

Why is God allowing it?

God will allow us free will. Also, if God is allowing something, He is using it. It is up to the person who feels aggrieved how they will behave or misbehave as to whether and when God can intervene and send help from the Sanctuary. Even the woman who is left alone cannot act a fool. If both of you are in your flesh, you're both wrong and that will repel God.

Isaiah 54 is about the individual forsaken woman. *For the Lord hath called thee as a woman forsaken.* This shows that after suffering. After atonement. After justice, then comes restoration.

A woman forsaken, grieved in spirit, and refused. God does not rebuke her tears there. He names her condition. Naming precedes healing.

The Lord is in his holy temple, the Lord's throne is in heaven: his eyes behold, his eyelids try, the children of men. (Psalm 11:4)

God sees. God examines. God tests. He scrutinizes. He narrows His gaze. He evaluates not only the tears, not only the abandonment, not only the public narrative and shame. He sees motive. He tests hearts.

The Lord is in His Holy temple. His throne is in Heaven. His eyes behold everything. Nothing in covenant is hidden from Him--, not the vow, not the violation, not the tears, the motive, or the Treachery.

The Lord is still on His throne.

Put thou my tears into thy bottle: are they not in thy book? (Psalm 56:8)

David is speaking from distress — betrayal, fear, instability. And he says: You count my wanderings. You collect my tears. You record them.

God does not waste tears; neither does. He ignore them. He does not forget them. Notice something important: The verse does not say God immediately stops the tears. It says He **stores** them.

God sees tears — including the ones caused by covenant violation--, maybe especially those, since covenant should have been a pre-answer to trouble, worry, loss, fears and tears. As well, God sees who **caused** the covenant destruction. That is judicial. God says: ***I saw it.*** That's your caution. There is a witness--, at least one.

Isaiah 54 shows the forsaken wife. Psalm 56 shows God storing tears. Malachi 2 says something very direct: "The Lord hath been witness between thee and the wife of thy youth, against whom thou hast dealt treacherously"

And then: "…he regardeth not the offering any more…"

If a man is the **cause** of tears through treachery, the text already tells us that God is witness. God weighs. God does not ignore.

If you have caused those tears through faithlessness, know this: they were not shed just in private; God sees. God saw. The Lord is witness between you and the wife of your youth. He sees what was vowed. He sees what was violated. He sees what was dismissed.

This is not threat; it is Truth.

That does not make the man a villain; It makes him accountable. If you will not keep a vow, do not make it. This is why nearly every marriage ceremony says something about do not enter into this union lightly. Breaking covenant, breaking a vow invites the devil into a person's life. Often, that's when things start going wrong or really wrong and it is not by the hand of the woman who was left of abandoned. It is Scriptural. There is a judgment for breaking covenant, especially unrepented.

Accountability is not cruelty. It is covenant. I am cautioning against treachery.

No matter what side you're on now or what side you've been on, the same God who sees her tears also sees his repentance.

Honor Is a Command, Not a Sentiment

Adult children are morally bound to aging parents, and Scripture treats neglect as a faith issue, not a family preference. Abandonment does not only occur in marriage. It also occurs quietly, steadily, and devastatingly between generations.

Few things are more normalized in modern life than adult children distancing themselves from aging parents. Distance is reframed as independence. Neglect is softened into busyness. Silence is justified as self-care.

Scripture does not accept these explanations.

In the Bible, honor toward parents does not expire when childhood ends. It deepens. Honor is not affection. It is not agreement. It is not nostalgia. Honor is obligation.

When Scripture commands honor, it is commanding active responsibility, not warm feeling. This is why the command appears not as advice, but as law. In Exodus, honoring father and mother is embedded in the moral structure of society itself. It is the only commandment paired with a promise—not because it is easy, but because it is foundational.

Honor is how continuity is protected.

Adult children are not exempt. Modern culture treats adulthood as release from obligation. Scripture treats adulthood as assumption of responsibility. When parents age, weaken, or become inconvenient, the Bible does not say:

- “Follow your peace.”
- “Protect your energy.”
- “You owe nothing now.”

It says the opposite. In 1 Timothy, care for aging family members is described as a test of faith itself. Neglect is not framed as unfortunate; it is framed as denial. This is severe language, and it is intentional.

Distance does not cancel duty. Geography has always changed. Obligation has not. Scripture never ties honor to proximity. It ties honor to relationship.

Distance may alter how care is expressed, but it does not erase responsibility. Phone calls, advocacy, financial support, presence when it matters—these are modern equivalents of ancient obligations.

Neglect dressed up as logistics is still neglect.

Aging parents become vulnerable. Aging reverses dependence. Those who once provided now require care. Those who once guided now need guidance. Those who once sacrificed now rely on others’ faithfulness. This reversal is not failure; it is life. Scripture assumes this moment will come. That is why it prepares children—not parents—for it.

The lie of "they'll be fine" is wishful thinking at best. One of the most damaging justifications for neglect is reassurance without responsibility. "They're strong." "They have resources." "They don't need me."

Scripture never excuses abandonment based on assumed resilience.

God consistently sides with those who are overlooked precisely because others assume someone else will notice. Care is not delegated by assumption.

This chapter does not deny that some relationships are broken by abuse or profound harm. Scripture does not demand closeness where safety is violated. But Scripture also does not permit casual estrangement to masquerade as righteousness.

There is a difference between boundaries that protect and distance that excuses neglect. Scripture discerns that difference by fruit, not language. When estrangement results in abandonment, Scripture calls it what it is.

This matters to God because parents represent history. They embody continuity. They carry memory. To discard them is to declare that usefulness determines worth.

God rejects this logic outright.

This is why Scripture repeatedly warns against forgetting those who can no longer repay.

The generational consequence is that neglect is learned. Children who watch parents abandon grandparents are being trained—even unintentionally—to do the same.

Scripture understands this generational transmission. Honor is commanded not only to protect the elderly, but to preserve the moral future. What is tolerated becomes tradition.

This book does not claim all parents were perfect. It does not deny pain or complexity. It insists on this Imperfection does not nullify obligation. Inconvenience does not erase duty. And adulthood does not cancel honor.

Scripture is not naïve about family difficulty. It is firm about family responsibility. Honor is active, not emotional. Adult children remain morally bound. Distance does not equal exemption. Neglect is a spiritual issue, not a lifestyle choice. Care for aging parents is not charity. It is covenantal faithfulness.

Right Prayers

There is a way to pray when you have been dealt treacherously with. There is a way not to. Some prayers shrink the soul. Some strengthen it. Some are rooted in shame. Some are rooted in justice.

Do not pray self-blame prayers. Do not pray, "Lord, show me what I did to deserve this." Do not pray: "Fix me so he won't leave." Do not pray: "Make me more desirable." Do not pray, "Help me compete." Do not pray asking for help in being less difficult, or a burden.

Treachery is not corrected by self-erasure. A person left you and no matter in what state they left you—they left you, not God. They broke covenant and you are not responsible for another person's breach of covenant. Examination is wise. Self-condemnation is not.

Prayers for Justice

Justice is not revenge. Justice is alignment. It is okay to pray, "Lord, bring what is hidden into light." "Lord, judge between us rightly." "Lord, protect what is righteous." "Lord, expose what is false."

Justice prayer says, "I trust You to weigh this."

These are appropriate style prayers to pray:

Prayers for Mercy. Prayers for Grace.

Prayers for Covering. Covering is not hiding. It is protection. Pray, Father: “Guard my heart.” “Guard my children.” “Guard my speech.” “Guard my dignity.” “Guard me from bitterness.” Covering keeps pain from multiplying.

Prayers for Provision. If covenant is shaken, fear often follows. Pray: “Lord, provide stability.” “Lord, provide Wisdom.” “Father, give me strength.” “Lord, provide what I cannot manufacture.” Provision prayer refuses panic.

Prayers for Guidance and Divine opportunities.

Prayers for Accountability. This is the mature prayer. “Lord, hold him accountable.” Not: “Destroy him.” But, “Do not let treachery prosper.” “Correct what is crooked.” “Bring conviction.” Accountability belongs to God. You do not need to execute justice. You entrust it.

Right prayers do not beg for manipulation. They align with righteousness. Right prayers do not attempt to control outcomes. They entrust outcomes to God. Right prayers do not erase pain; they keep pain from becoming corruption.

God as Defender, Not Bystander

Scripture repeatedly positions God on the side of the abandoned—and why that should sober everyone else.

One of the most persistent lies about God is that He merely observes. That He watches quietly. That He sympathizes but does not intervene, or that He is present in theory but absent in practice.

Scripture dismantles this idea decisively. God does not describe Himself as a bystander to abandonment. He names Himself as Defender. God chooses sides—intentionally. Throughout Scripture, God consistently aligns Himself with those who lack leverage. Not because they are flawless. Not because they are always right. But because they are vulnerable. Widows. The aged. The left, the abandoned, the forgotten. Marginalized, disenfranchised. Those pushed aside when usefulness diminishes.

God does not hover neutrally between parties when covenant is broken. He moves—deliberately—toward the one who was wronged.

This should sober anyone tempted to treat abandonment as a private decision.

Defender of Widows is a title. When Scripture calls God a defender of widows, it is not offering comfort language. It is declaring jurisdiction. A defender hears cases, investigates wrongdoing, and intervenes on behalf of the injured. This is why Scripture repeatedly warns against mistreating widows, the aged, and the dependent. The warning is not emotional, it is legal.

To abandon the vulnerable is not merely to disappoint them. It is to place oneself in opposition to God's chosen role.

God steps in when humans step away**.** Abandonment often creates a vacuum. Support disappears. Advocacy dissolves. Presence evaporates.

Scripture repeatedly shows that God moves *into* these vacuums. When people withdraw protection, God supplies it. When people withdraw provision, God accounts for it. When people withdraw memory, God remembers.

This is why Scripture speaks so forcefully about forgetting the widow or neglecting the aged. God treats forgetfulness as a moral act, not an accident.

Divine memory is an act of justice. In the Bible, to "remember" is not merely to recall—it is to act. When God remembers someone, He moves on their behalf. Human beings forget when someone no longer serves their interests. God remembers precisely those people. This difference is not sentimental. It is judicial.

God's memory restores dignity where humans erase it.

God's defense often seems delayed. One of the most difficult realities for the abandoned is delay. Those who leave often appear to prosper. Those left behind often struggle. Logistically, the person who leaves planned to leave. The one who stayed was left flat footed. The one who leaves is not always, but can be corrupt so their future successes may be by corrupt means. If the victim was a corrupt person, they might not be a victim, but they'd be corrupt. Which is worse, to be poor or a liar?

> The desire of a man is his kindness: and a poor man is better than a liar. (Proverbs 19:22)

Scripture does not deny this tension. It explains it.

God's justice is not rushed—but it is exact. Delay is not absence. It is restraint. God allows space for repentance, but He does not lose record. Every act of abandonment is weighed with precision.

This is why Scripture consistently warns against mistaking silence for approval. There is danger in being on the wrong side of God's defense. When God identifies Himself as Defender, it implies something uncomfortable: There is an opposing side.

Those who abandon the vulnerable are not merely making personal choices. They are positioning themselves against God's declared interest.

This does not mean God refuses Mercy. It means Mercy does not erase accountability. Scripture never suggests that forgiveness cancels consequence. It insists that repentance precedes restoration.

This matters for those who fear being left, This chapter is not written to romanticize suffering; it is written to anchor truth. If people abandon you, God does not. If people forget you, God remembers. If people erase you, God records you.

This is not wishful thinking. It is covenant reality. God's defense may not look like immediate reversal, but it always looks like presence, provision, and preservation.

This matters for those tempted to leave. This chapter also speaks a warning. Abandonment is never isolated; it always enters a courtroom. Even when no human authority intervenes, God does. To abandon someone who depended on you is to create a case God has already agreed to hear. If it never goes to a civil court, it will still go to the Courts of Heaven, and especially if the wounded party takes it there. When that wounded woman reports to Heaven what happened and who did what and her current predicament, Jehovah Roi will investigate and intervene.

God's defense of the vulnerable does not mean He infantilizes them. It means He refuses to let injustice stand. He does not erase their agency. He restores their dignity. He does not negotiate with betrayal.

God is not neutral toward abandonment. Defense is a Divine role. It is not a human projection. Forgetting is a moral act. Delay does not equal indifference. God does not hover when covenant is violated. He steps in.

That reality changes how abandonment must be understood.

Justice Is Not Cruelty

One of the most effective ways injustice survives in the natural world is by redefining justice as harshness. Scripture does not apologize for judgment. We serve a God of balance.

Accountability is called unloving. Consequences are labeled as bitterness. Naming wrongdoing is framed as a lack of Grace. Scripture does not accept these definitions.

Justice is not cruelty. Justice is order restored.

Justice makes people uncomfortable. Justice unsettles those who benefit from disorder. It interrupts narratives that allow people to move on without reckoning. It disrupts the illusion that harm can be committed quietly and left behind.

Replacement culture prefers closure without consequence. Scripture insists on accountability before restoration. This difference is not philosophical; it is moral.

God's Justice is not emotional. Human justice often swings between extremes—either vengeance or avoidance. God's justice does neither. Scripture presents Divine justice as measured, deliberate, and precise. It is not fueled by anger. It is fueled by Truth.

God does not punish because He is offended. He intervenes because something has been violated. He steps in when covenant is broken. Justice is not personal; it is structural.

Consequences are not optional. Scripture never treats consequences as unkind. It treats them as corrective. Without consequence:

- betrayal multiplies
- loyalty weakens
- the vulnerable are taught they are unsafe

Justice is what stops harm from repeating. When consequences are removed in the name of Grace, Scripture calls it indulgence—not Mercy.

But they've moved on. This phrase often appears after abandonment. The one who left has rebuilt. The one left behind is still untangling loss. Scripture does not treat moving on as moral exoneration. Time passing does not equal resolution. New beginnings do not erase old obligations. Justice does not expire because someone appears happy.

God's justice accounts for what humans overlook. Human systems often fail to measure: emotional labor, years of sacrifice, unseen support, opportunities passed over or lost, and cost. God's justice accounts for all of it.

Nothing poured out in faithfulness is invisible to God. Nothing taken and discarded is forgotten. This is why Scripture repeatedly reassures the abandoned that God sees what others minimize.

Justice is often mistaken for bitterness. When the wounded speak truth, they are often accused of being bitter. Scripture distinguishes bitterness from clarity. Bitterness corrodes internally. Clarity confronts externally. Justice requires clarity. Refusing to name wrongdoing does not heal wounds. It deepens them.

Forgive and forget is a myth. Scripture never commands forgetting. God forgives, but He remembers. He restores, but He records. Forgiveness in Scripture is never the erasure of truth. It is the refusal to retaliate while justice is pursued rightly. To demand forgetting is to demand silence. Scripture never demands that.

Justice protects the vulnerable. Justice creates boundaries. It signals that betrayal has cost. It tells the vulnerable they are not disposable. It tells the strong they are not untouchable. Without justice, abandonment becomes normalized. God refuses this normalization.

Delayed justice is still justice. Scripture acknowledges that justice is often delayed—but never denied. Delay allows for repentance. It allows for change.

It allows for Mercy. But delay does not cancel reckoning. God's patience is not forgetfulness.

Justice is Truth named, responsibility assigned, and order restored. Justice is not revenge, cruelty, or public humiliation.

Scripture holds Justice and Mercy together without confusing them.

Justice is not unloving. Consequences are not cruelty. Forgiveness does not erase truth. Silence does not equal Peace. Justice is how God protects covenant. Where covenant is violated, Justice is not optional.

The Right Way to Pray

Scripture never teaches the vulnerable to pray for self-blame. Prayer must align with justice. Prayer reveals theology--, not the theology we claim, but the theology we actually believe. The way people pray about abandonment exposes where they think responsibility lies, who they think must change, and what kind of God they believe is listening.

Scripture is clear: prayer does not replace Justice; it aligns with it.

The wrong emphasis produces the wrong burden. Many prayers surrounding abandonment sound spiritual but quietly shift responsibility onto the vulnerable.

Prayers like:

- "Help me not to be left."
- "Help me stay valuable."
- "Help me not to lose favor."

These prayers are understandable. They are born of fear. But they are not how Scripture frames the issue. The

Bible does not train the vulnerable to pray against becoming victims. It trains the community to pray against becoming a culture of betrayers and *Leavers*.

Prayer is not a tool for self-blame. Scripture never uses prayer to reinforce shame. When prayer becomes self-surveillance, self-correction for someone else's sin, spiritual bargaining to prevent betrayal. it has departed from biblical alignment.

God does not ask the abandoned to fix what they did not break.

Biblical prayer names responsibility. The prayers of Scripture are strikingly direct. They ask for protection for the vulnerable, conviction for the unfaithful, restraint over desire, remembrance of covenant. Prayer is not neutral language. It calls things into alignment.

This is why many Biblical prayers sound confrontational—they are designed to confront disorder, not soothe it.

The vulnerable are invited to pray for covering, guidance, and protection where support has been withdrawn

- Provision — practical care, not just emotional relief
- Presence — companionship and advocacy
- Vindication — truth made visible
- Peace — not denial, but stability

These prayers do not ask God to prevent wrongdoing by self-erasure. They ask God to step into the gap created by abandonment.

The strong are responsible to pray with power. If in spiritual warfare, we put on the whole armor of God. We do not battle flesh and blood, we do not pray against them—we go higher, we are wrestling with spiritual powers in high places, but we still can be victorious. Scripture places prayer squarely in the hands of those with power.

Who are they?

They are the righteous. The prayers of the righteous make much **power** available to the pray-er. They are to pray for the fear of God, restraint of impulse, clarity of conscience, remembrance of vows, and the strength to remain faithful.

Prayer that does not confront desire is not prayer—it is indulgence.

Some prayers feel uncomfortable. Biblical prayer often makes people uneasy because it does not flatter. It names sin. It invites correction. It asks God to intervene. This discomfort is not a flaw; it is evidence that prayer is doing its work.

Pray prayers that align with GOD'S character.

Scripture consistently models prayer that aligns with God's roles, especially as the Judge who sees. He is the Defender who acts. God is the Father who remembers.

He is the Shepherd who protects. Prayer that ignores these attributes of God becomes thin and misdirected. To pray rightly is to pray in agreement with who God has declared Himself to be.

This book offers orientation. Prayer is not about controlling people. It is about submitting situations to God's order. Right prayer refuses to excuse betrayal and refuses to blame the wounded.

This chapter does not suggest prayer replaces boundaries, Wisdom, or action. Prayer is not passivity. It is participation with God's justice.

Prayer reveals belief. Self-blame is not spiritual. God does not require the vulnerable to **prevent** sin, especially the sin of others. Right prayer aligns with Justice. Prayer does not exist to keep Peace at the cost of Truth. It exists to call Heaven and Earth back into alignment.

What Loyalty Looks Like in Practice

Faithfulness should be lived quietly, consistently, and without applause. Loyalty is rarely dramatic. It does not announce itself. It does not trend. It does not receive the accolades of men. In Scripture, loyalty is proven not by declarations, but by **continuity**—the decision to **remain** when leaving would be easier, praised, or excused.

Loyalty is ordinary—and that is the point. Most betrayals are justified by extraordinary language:

- "This is my one life."
- "I deserve happiness."
- "I have to be true to myself."

Loyalty, by contrast, shows up in the ordinary:

- staying present
- keeping promises
- doing what no longer feels rewarding

Scripture never treats loyalty as heroic because it is flashy. It treats it as righteous because it is reliable.

Loyalty looks like staying when nothing is returned. One of the clearest markers of covenant faithfulness is this: The willingness to remain when reciprocity disappears. When energy is gone. When affirmation is absent. When gratitude is inconsistent. Replacement culture says, *leave*. Scripture says, *remain*—unless remaining enables harm.

Loyalty is not blind endurance. It is steadfast responsibility.

Loyalty includes presence, not just provision. Many people confuse loyalty with material support. Provision matters—but presence matters more. Loyalty looks like showing up consistently, being reachable, advocating when someone cannot advocate for themselves, staying engaged when withdrawal would be easier.

Scripture does not allow people to outsource faithfulness while emotionally disappearing.

Absence with a check attached is still absence.

Loyalty honors history. Loyalty remembers what was built together. Loyalty remembers years of shared labor, memories made, sacrifices that cannot be repaid, and seasons that required trust.

Scripture treats history as binding, not disposable. To erase shared history in order to justify departure is not clarity; it is revision. Loyalty does not rewrite the past to excuse the present.

Loyalty is visible in small decisions. Faithfulness is not proven in crisis alone. It is proven in repetition. In returning calls, checking in, refusing to emotionally disengage, protecting someone's dignity when they are not present.

Loyalty is practiced long before it is tested.

Loyalty protects dignity. One of the most overlooked aspects of loyalty is how someone is spoken about after seasons change.

Loyalty does not mock aging, minimize sacrifice, or reframe faithfulness as foolishness.

Scripture treats dignity as something to be guarded—not negotiated. Even when relationships are strained, loyalty refuses to humiliate.

Loyalty requires restraint. Loyalty is not passive. It requires saying no. No to impulse. No to comparison. No to narratives that excuse departure.

Scripture repeatedly praises restraint—not as repression, but as strength.

Anyone can follow desire. Few are willing to govern it.

Loyalty is costly—and Scripture never denies this. The Bible never pretends loyalty is easy. It acknowledges fatigue, disappointment, and unfulfilled expectations. But it does not conclude that difficulty nullifies obligation.

Instead, Scripture consistently frames endurance as evidence of character. Cost does not invalidate covenant; it confirms it.

Loyalty is quietly observed by God. Much of loyalty goes unseen by people. But Scripture insists it is not unseen by God. God watches who stays, who remembers, who remains faithful when no one is watching. He does not confuse loud declarations with lived obedience.

Loyalty matters. Loyalty stabilizes families. It anchors communities. It protects the vulnerable. Without loyalty, covenant collapses into convenience.

Scripture refuses to allow that collapse.

Loyalty is practical, not performative. Presence matters as much as provision. Dignity is part of faithfulness. Restraint is strength. Endurance is not weakness. Loyalty is not proven in youth. It is proven over time, and Scripture still honors it.

Known By Your Soul

Earlier we said that a person must love your soul to really connect with you in any lasting and Godly way. This is not by seduction or by performance, or by vulnerability theater. But this must be as integrity. Before someone can love your soul, your soul has to be visible. Your real soul must be visible, not something curated, managed, armored, decorated or diluted.

To know someone's soul is to be known. Deeply known.

To be known by your soul, you must stop auditioning. To be known by your soul, you must let someone see what steadies you, not just what impresses you. To be known by your soul, you must resist the urge to shrink to remain liked.

To be known by your soul, you must first be honest with yourself.

1. Genesis — we see the word, *cleave***.** Genesis 2:24:

"Therefore shall a man leave his father and his mother, and shall cleave unto his wife…"

“Cleave” there means to cling, to adhere, to stick fast, to be joined in covenant loyalty. It is not casual attachment. It is binding attachment. It implies exclusivity, durability, and covenantal fusion. It is not romance language. It is structural language.

2. David & Jonathan — “The souls of Jonathan and David were knit” 1 Samuel 18:1:

“…the soul of Jonathan was knit with the soul of David…”

Different context. That is covenant friendship. Political loyalty. Mutual risk. Deep affection. But not marriage. Still, notice the word: Knit. Bound. Interwoven.

Both passages speak of adhesion at the level of soul.

Playing Together or Staying Together?

People 'play' marriage in relationships when there is no covenant at all (maybe only entanglement or soul tie). Then there are those who *play* marriage because they have not covenanted.

Sometimes they have not covenanted with the person, but their covenant is with what that person has or can do for them.

Covenant implies permanence and permanence changes behavior. When permanence is assumed, you invest differently. You speak differently. You endure differently. You resolve conflict differently. You don't keep one foot near the exit. When permanence is not assumed, you perform. You negotiate. You manage optics. You hedge your bets. You extract while you can.

Some people don't covenant with the person. They covenant with what the person provides. A person can be loyal to comfort, money, status, beauty, admiration, security, sexual access, emotional supply and calling any of that, "love."

But that's not covenant with a soul. That's covenant with benefit. When the benefit changes, the "covenant" dissolves. Which means it was never covenant. It was agreement of convenience.

Modern relationships often attempt soul-level intensity without covenantal structure. People move in together. They share finances, bodies, secrets, trauma and daily life. Many times, they do all this without vows, and without plans for permanence, and all without structure. They simulate marriage.

A marriage simulation does not make a covenant or even simulate one. Simulation does create attachment. Attachment feels like cleaving, but without covenant, it's entanglement. Entanglements can feel like soul. But it lacks anchor.

Remember, every strong attachment is neither Divine nor demonic; it could be either. You yourself, for yourself need to distinguish. Is this psychological bonding, physical/sexual bonding, trauma bonding, spiritual alignment, covenant union, or hormonal needs or rewards such as with dopamine or oxytocin?

True covenantal cleaving requires leaving prior allegiances. A public vow. Moral alignment. Mutual endurance. Willing transformation. If those elements are missing, intensity alone does not qualify.

Modern culture often worships emotion while neglecting structure.

Permanence doesn't automatically mean the relationship is healthy. Some people remain permanently in dysfunction. Covenant requires righteousness, not just duration. Covenant is necessary for stability, but covenant must be aligned with God to be life-giving.

How can you know which it is?

If a man makes a statement that he claims to be prophetic and says God said it and it turns out to be true, then that man made a prophetic statement. if it proves untrue, then it is not a prophetic statement from God. TIME is the judge, not feelings, not appearances, not their nice house or how many kids they have. TIME.

A stable nuclear family has a mother and father, a husband and a wife who have *cleaved* to one another. There are married parents in the traditional home structure. Predictable moral order, representing staying, parental presence, predictability, structure.

Cleave in Genesis is covenantal obligation. Soul knit in Samuel is voluntary devotion.

Extraction and simulation relationships *mimic* cleaving without covenant. Without covenant means there is no vow made and no semblance of covenant, but it can also mean that both parties are not in the covenant. One could be very sincere and serious and the other just going through the motions. Meaning: There is one person in the marriage.

Some men simulate cleaving while they are only sampling and biding time. Well, they are biding their time; they are wasting the time of the woman they are sampling.

Cleave without covenant is counterfeit adhesion.

If a person does not know you at the level of soul, *what* are they loving?

If someone does not know your convictions, your fears, your moral boundaries what do they know about you, really? If they don't know your grief history, thought patterns, your relationship with God--, therefore your spiritual boundaries, then what are they attached to?

Two-way street: Do you know their soul? Have you both been mutually open and available to one another?

Usually it's one or more of the following: your body, your energy, your usefulness (to include your money or wealth), your admiration, your personality, your compliance. All of these things are temporal in that they can change tomorrow.

Uusefulness includes emotional labor, sexual availability, admiration, stability, reputation, domestic contribution, and of course, money. A person can be loved for their access to resources just as easily as for their body. That does not make them foolish. It means someone saw value and treated it transactionally.

Carnal attachment is volatile because it is based on shifting features.

Soul-level love is stable because it is anchored in identity, not performance. So, when those carnal things change, a man who was never attached to the soul feels justified moving on.

Okay, so is the "God-joined" marriage a soul-level union?

When Jesus says, "What God has joined together…"that joining is covenantal. It is not merely emotional intensity. It is not just chemistry. It is not trauma bonding. It is not just shared goals because you both want a big house in the suburbs or a slick penthouse in the city. It is definitely not sexual bonding; lust lasts on the average two years. After that time, you may find that one or both of you are serial 'daters.

Next!

A God-joined marriage is Divine recognition of a covenant vow. A soul-level Divine union would include shared submission to God, shared moral framework, shared covenant understanding, and shared ideals of permanence. Without covenant, strong emotional or sexual bonding can mimic soul connection.

Mimicry is not marriage.

When God is in it, it is covenant. "God is in it" does not mean it feels powerful or the ceremony was in a church. It doesn't mean that it feels destined, necessarily. It may feel spiritual but other entities besides God can bring on *spiritual* feelings. This is why I capitalize words such as Divine and Angels so you, Dear Reader can know I'm talking about God's side of the equation and not just anything spiritual, related to any kind of deity, or about any kind of angels.

When God is in it, that means it aligns with Scripture. It honors covenant. It produces Peace, not erosion. It protects both souls. It does not require compromise of conscience. God does not join what destroys a person. God joins what can endure.

Soul ties — real vs counterfeit. There are attachments that feel deep but are not Divine. Some examples are trauma bonds, sexual bonding without covenant, shared crisis attachment, manipulative intensity, and spiritualized infatuation. All these can feel "soul-level" but they are not covenant.

They are entanglements. Thankfully, entanglements can be broken. Through Truth, repentance, boundaries, separation and distance, and even sometimes grief.

Covenant, once entered legitimately, is not dissolved by emotion.

Flesh, carnal, temporal, transient, insincere attachments are unstable. Emotional intensity is also unstable. Extraction relationships, those who came to take are also unstable. Trauma bonds and pain cliques are unstable.

The only thing that is stable is Covenant. Godly, Divine covenants. Unless purposefully broken in the spirit realm, covenants remain forever.

Soul-level knowledge + covenant is enduring

Depth alone does not make a connection Divine. Many people go deep quickly. True covenant is not measured by intensity. It is measured by permanence, integrity, and obedience to God.

Arranged marriages? Glad you asked that. Since time immemorial there have been arranged marriages; we see them throughout the Bible and even in our modern times. Many last, even involving people who have never met.

Arranged marriages —how do they stay together? Is it fear or obedience? Neither, necessarily. Historically, arranged marriages operated from family covenant, economic alignment, social stability, and shared belief system. communal accountability. Love was expected to grow inside covenant.

Modern Western culture reversed the order: feel deeply and that would lead to covenant. Traditional systems often did, making covenant first, then growing deeply.

The problem is that a person cannot bear their soul all at once, so one cannot know a person suddenly or all at once, nor should they want to. Soul exposure is progressive. It requires safety, time, demonstrated integrity, and observed patterns. If someone demands immediate vulnerability, that is not soul love. That is acceleration. And acceleration often hides instability. Soul-level love takes time.

Cleave means both to separate and to join. In Hebrew, "cleave" (*dabaq*) means to cling, adhere, and stick fast. Cleaving also has that paradox in English: To cleave can mean to split. And that is fascinating symbolically. Marriage involves Leaving (separating from prior loyalties), cleaving (attaching to new covenant).

There is a tearing before there is a binding. You do not become one without separation from something else. When two people **willingly** endure that process the leaving, the rearranging, the exposure, the adjustment, the dying to prior self-protection, that is when stabilization happens.

I am not implying that any intense soul bond is God-joined. A God-joined union is marked by Covenant vow, shared submission to God, mutual transformation (conversion), endurance through separation and reattachment, and this will show as stability under stress.

Intensity alone does not equal Divine joining. Endurance + obedience does.

Attachment is easy. Exposure is progressive. Cleaving requires separation. Covenant requires will. Soul love requires time. Stability requires obedience.

Covenant vs. Simulation: Time is the audit. Not intensity. Not aesthetic. Not "they look happy. Not how many children. Not how many Bible verses. Not how convincing the testimony. Time reveals what was structure and what was scaffolding.

Not every relationship that looks like marriage is covenant. Some are simulations. They may share a home, a bed, finances. They may share children. They may even share language about God.

But sharing is not the same as covenant. Covenant is not proven by proximity; it is proven by permanence under pressure. Permanence is not measured in months. It is measured in time. Time tests everything. Time tests loyalty. Time tests motives. Time tests whether someone loved a soul or simply benefited from a season.

Simulation looks like urgency without vow. It is intimacy without accountability. It is access without permanence. It is shared life without public commitment. It is destiny talk without structure. It is high emotion with low endurance. Simulation often feels powerful.

It may even feel spiritual, but it resists structure. It avoids binding language. It postpones clarity. It keeps one exit unsealed.

Covenant looks like public vow, mutual leaving of prior allegiances. Accountability before God and community. Endurance during inconvenience. Alignment of moral framework. Willing transformation over time. Covenant does not panic when seasons change.

It does not renegotiate loyalty every time feelings fluctuate. It does not disappear when benefit decreases.

The test of time: If a man says, "God told me," time will tell. If he says, "I will never leave," time will tell. If he says, "You are my wife and my heart," time will tell.

Time exposes whether the covenant was with the person or with what the person provided. A man can covenant with comfort. A man can covenant with beauty. A man can covenant with money. A man can covenant with admiration. When those change, so does his loyalty. That was not covenant; that was arrangement.

When God joins something, it stabilizes. Not instantly, not effortlessly. But it does not collapse under ordinary strain. There is fruit over time. There is consistency. There is integrity between words and behavior. Not perfection. Consistency.

Intensity is not covenant. Sex is not covenant (but it does create soul ties). Shared trauma is not covenant. Living together is not covenant. Private promises are not covenant. Public vow + alignment + endurance = covenant. And the judge of whether it was real is not how it looked in year one. It is what remains in year ten. Time is the judge.

God Hates Broken Covenant

God hates divorce. (Malachi 2)

But that same passage says men dealt treacherously. So, God really **hates treachery.** He hates covenant treated lightly. He hates violence done to trust. He does not hate the wounded spouse. He does not hate repentance. He does not hate restoration. He hates faithlessness.

Covenant**:** sacred but violable. A covenant is sacred because it binds two people before God. It is violable because humans have free will. God's hatred of broken covenant is not hatred of the person. It is hatred of treachery, seen in the willful betrayal of what was vowed.

So**,** what happens when covenant is violated?

Three truths hold at the same time:

1. The violation is real.
2. The covenant is still sacred.
3. Restoration is possible, but not automatic.

Forgiveness is immediate in the heart. Trust is rebuilt in time. Time is still the judge.

Do not treat covenant lightly. It is better to never make a vow than to make one and not fulfill it. If someone steps out from covenant, they cannot re-enter with flowers, tears, jewelry, and dramatic apologies. Yeah, all that will get you back in the **house**, but to get back in right standing you must be sure you are back and securely in covenant. Some people renew their vows publicly, some privately. Especially be sure to repent to God.

A person can re-enter back into covenant by confession without excuse. They need to also sever the external attachment. They can enter back in with transparency, submission, and accountability. They then demonstrate consistency over time.

Sometimes repentance comes too late. Sometimes the wound is too deep.

Scripture allows for dissolution under certain conditions. That is not rebellion; that is acknowledgment of violation. Dissolution should never be casual because covenant was never casual.

A man who loves your soul does not treat covenant lightly. A man who covenants with benefits, or simulates for the benefits, will break faith when benefit changes.

The man who covenants with money is the employee. if the boss stops paying either what he agreed to or what the man wants--- he quits the 'job. Employment is transactional. If a man's loyalty is anchored to income, comfort, lifestyle, admiration, status, or sexual access; he is not a husband in covenant. He is a contractor. When the compensation shifts, he renegotiates or resigns. That is not treachery in business. It is treachery in covenant on one or both sides.

Marriage is not an employment agreement. It is not: "I stay while this benefits me." It is: "I stay because I vowed before God." A man who covenants before God will tremble before violating that vow.

God hates treachery, but He restores the treacherous when they repent. He defends the betrayed. And He does not confuse violation with permanence.

There is the woman who stayed too long**.** Staying is not always righteousness. Sometimes staying is because of fear, financial dependence, confusion, spiritual pressure, hope without evidence, misunderstanding covenant

Covenant requires two. If one party repeatedly violates, refuses repentance, refuses accountability, and continues treachery — the other party is not obligated to pretend covenant exists. Endurance is noble. Self-erasure is not. Staying too long is not loyalty if there is no repentance to respond to.

Many women stayed because they believed God wanted them to.

The woman who left. Leaving is not always rebellion. Sometimes leaving is acknowledgment of violation. Sometimes it is for the protection of children. It could be the refusal to normalize treachery. It could be the recognition that covenant has been desecrated repeatedly. Leaving must never be casual.

If she left because feelings faded, boredom grew, comparison tempted, greener grass beckoned. Then that is not discernment. That is instability. Time will judge that too. Time is the judge. Not flowers. Not new rings. Not Instagram apologies. Not sudden church attendance.

Time.

If he repents and stays consistent under scrutiny for years — that speaks. If he repents for two weeks and reverts — that speaks too. If she leaves and builds a life of integrity and peace — that speaks.

If she leaves and repeats the same pattern — that speaks as well. Time exposes covenant. Time exposes simulation. Time exposes whether the soul was loved or merely consumed.

A man who covenants with money will leave when payment changes. A man who covenants with admiration will leave when admiration fades. A man who covenants with beauty will leave when beauty shifts. But a man who covenants before God understands that he does not own the covenant and remain accountable to it.

The soul does not age. it can mature but it will never look old. the soul does not gain or lose weight; it can prosper but it remains the beautiful soul it was when you two met. the one who loves your soul and is covenanted with God in the cords will stay. (I have found him whom my soul loveth.) A threefold cord is not easily broken. She's a beautiful soul, as beautiful as the day we met (some may say).

The soul does not age. The body changes. The face lines. The hair grays. The waist shifts. The strength fluctuates. But the soul does not wrinkle The soul does not sag. The soul does not gain or lose weight. The soul does not depreciate in value. It can mature. It can deepen. It can scar. It can heal. But it does not age.

The Lord restores my soul. (Psalm 23)

That is why loving the body alone is unstable. The body is guaranteed to change. The soul guarantees continuity.

"I Have Found Him Whom My Soul Loveth" Song of Songs is not infatuation language. It is recognition language. Not, "I found the one who excites me." But "I found the one whom my soul loveth." That implies depth, discernment, alignment, recognition beyond surface. It is not hormonal; it is anchored.

The Threefold Cord.

A threefold cord is not quickly broken. (Ecclesiastes 4:12)

Two people alone can fray. Two people bound before God introduce a third strand. But be careful here. The threefold cord is not: Him + Her + Intensity. It is: Him + Her + God.

Remove God, and you have only two strands. Two strands under strain eventually thin. Three strands distribute pressure.

"She's as beautiful as the day we met." That line only makes sense if he loved the soul from the beginning. Because if he loved youth, novelty, admiration, external shine, then time will contradict him. But if he loved integrity, mind, courage, conviction, character. Then time reveals more beauty, not less. Because the soul matures.

The woman on the cover of this book is not beautiful because she defied aging. She is beautiful because her soul endured. The man who loves her soul does not panic when seasons change. He recognizes her. Recognition is different from attraction. Attraction can be replaced. Recognition cannot.

This is not fantasy theology, it is covenant anthropology

People who end up in divorce court think the judge is divorcing them spiritually and on a soul level, like that judge is handling everything. Even the one whose left alone must be whole and alone, not pining away, soul tied, still entangled, etc; the judge can't do that. The ***Leaver*** probably doesn't know this any more than the ***Cleaver*** (the one who stayed).

The Judge is not divorcing you spiritually.

Even if your spouse left you all alone and took you to court, there is more to divorce than the judge with the gavel.

Many people speak of covenant violation as if a human judge dissolved the soul. They behave as if a signed and notarized paper in the natural dissolved the union. Well, in the natural it did, but how about in the spirit. How can a natural act sever a spiritual reality?

A civil judge handles legality. God handles covenant. And even then, God does not dissolve souls; He judges conduct. This is critical for the woman left alone, because many women think that if he left, something spiritual has been torn from them.

Not necessarily.

Covenant violation wounds. It does not amputate the soul. Your soul is not split in court. It is not parceled. It is not repossessed.

The woman left alone must become and remain whole. Ideally, she should have been whole all along, but this is especially important now. It doesn't matter her age, this is incumbent on her, not because she was never wounded, but because her soul was never owned.

If she remains pining, spiritually fused, tied, or entangled, rehearsing old vows, emotionally suspended (stuck), still orbiting his decisions, then she is not honoring covenant. She is maintaining entanglement which is not covenant.

There is a difference between grieving a covenant and remaining tied to someone who abandoned it.

Grief is healthy.

Bondage is not.

The Leaver probably doesn't know this any more than the Cleaver. The one who left may think "I made a new life. I moved on." But if covenant was real, time will expose whether he severed treachery, or merely relocated it.

The one who stayed may think "My endurance guarantees righteousness." Endurance without Truth can become self-erasure. Both sides can misunderstand covenant. Both sides can mistake attachment for soul unity. Both sides can confuse emotion with spiritual reality.

Time still judges both.

Covenant is not dissolved by mood. It is not rewritten by desire. It is not erased by attraction elsewhere. But neither is a wounded soul required to live forever in suspended animation. If covenant is violated and repentance refused, separation may occur. When separation occurs, the soul must not remain chained to treachery. You may grieve what was vowed. You may mourn what was broken, but you must not worship what left.

Your soul belongs to God first.

I will mention how to untie a soul tie and how to untangle from an entanglement -- very briefly because there are very excellent books on those subjects that have been penned and published already by this author; links in the credits.

Untying a Soul Tie

Not every deep attachment is covenant. Some are formed through intimacy without vow. Trauma shared without healing. Secrecy. Dependency. repeated emotional exposure. sexual bonding. When a relationship ends but the attachment persists, what lingers is not always love.

Sometimes it is imprint. Sometimes it is habit. Sometimes it is unfinished longing. Untying begins with Truth. You name it correctly. It is not destiny. It is not what God has joined. If there was no covenant, call it what it was: Attachment Entanglement. Evil soul tie. Experience.

Seek Truth because Truth weakens illusion.

Untying continues with complete, not partial separation. Not friendly orbiting—*let's remain friends.* If two you are co-parenting that is one thing, else --- why? No spiritualized check-ins. No, separation. You cannot untie a knot while continuing to pull on the string.

Then comes discipline. You refuse to rehearse old conversations, remembering *when.* Don't imagine reconciliations. Don't rehearse alternative endings or private nostalgia. The mind sustains what the heart is trying to release.

Untying is not instantaneous. It is by your repeated refusal to return to that same situation. Trust this: opportunities will be presented to your mind. Over time, the emotional charge diminishes. Time again becomes the judge.

Untangling from Entanglement is deeper than attraction but lighter than covenant. It feels weighty. It feels spiritual and binding, but it lacks vow.

Untangling requires a decision. Set and keep boundaries. Accountability. Redirection of attention. Reorientation toward God.

If repentance is required, repent. If forgiveness is required, forgive. If grief is required, grieve, but do not over grieve, pine away or dramatize the process. Untangling is rarely loud. It is quiet, repeated obedience. Over time, the soul regains equilibrium.

Covenant cannot be casually dissolved, but counterfeit bonds can be severed. The difference is not intensity, it is vow.

It is discernment. This book is not a formula for preventing someone from leaving you. It is not a strategy for securing a spouse. It is not a guarantee against betrayal.

There is no checklist that can override another person's will. This book does not promise control. It calls for discernment—your own discernment. Not your momma's or your best friend's – yours. You are the one in the relationship every day. You cannot contact someone to know what to do from moment to moment within your relationship.

Discernment requires you to evaluate your own relationship honestly — not through fear, not through fantasy, not through public appearances — but through fruit over time.

Do not dismay: there are genuine people in this world. But there are also performers. Some love deeply and covenantally. Some study, adapt, and act. No book can eliminate that reality. But clarity can reduce confusion. Time reveals what performance cannot sustain.

There is no checklist that can override another person's free will. No book can eliminate human freedom.

This book does not promise control. It calls for discernment. Discernment requires you to evaluate your relationship honestly — not through fear, fantasy, not through appearances — but through fruit over time.

There are good people who fail. Failure does not automatically mean malice. But repeated treachery is not immaturity — it is character.

A Warning and a Promise

What does Scripture say to those tempted to abandon—and to those who fear they will be left? Scripture rarely ends with ambiguity.

When a matter carries moral weight, God speaks with clarity—both to those tempted to do harm and to those who fear it may be done to them.

Abandonment is one of those matters.

This chapter does not soften what has been said. It brings it to completion.

A warning to those tempted to leave. Scripture does not deny temptation. It confronts it. Desire will come. Restlessness will whisper. Justifications will sound reasonable. But Scripture is unyielding on this point: Temptation explains nothing. It excuses nothing.

To abandon someone who depended on you is not a private decision. It is a public moral act with spiritual consequence.

God is not persuaded by better language. He is not confused by cultural approval. He is not absent from the record. What you call "moving on," Scripture may call **treachery**. God judges with accuracy, not sentiment.

For those who fear being left: Scripture does not dismiss fear. It answers it. To those who worry they will be forgotten when they weaken, age, or lose leverage, God speaks repeatedly and plainly: You are seen. You are remembered. You are defended. Not because you were perfect. Covenant matters to God even when it was broken by others.

Human loyalty may fail. Divine faithfulness does not.

God's accounting is complete. One of the most dangerous lies surrounding abandonment is that it goes unnoticed.

Scripture insists otherwise.

God accounts for years of unseen labor. He rewards sacrifices no one thanked you for. He has seen all your faithfulness that outlasted applause. Nothing poured out in good faith is lost. Nothing taken and discarded is erased.

God's memory is exact.

Justice and Mercy meet here. This book has spoken plainly about justice. It now speaks plainly about Mercy. Mercy is available—but not without Truth. Repentance does not mean rewriting history. It means acknowledging it. Restoration does not mean pretending harm never happened. It means responsibility is taken seriously.

God offers Mercy without diminishing justice. He offers forgiveness without denying consequence.

A Word on worth: Replacement culture teaches that worth diminishes with time. Scripture teaches the opposite. Worth deepens with faithfulness. Dignity is not lost with age. Covenant does not dissolve because the season has changed. If someone treated you as disposable, that judgment did not come from God.

But God has not missed it. Vengeance belongs to the Lord.

How To Be Known By Your Soul

Not as seduction.
Not as performance.
Not as vulnerability theater.

But as integrity.

Because here's the turn:

Before someone can love your soul,
your soul has to be visible.

Not curated.
Not managed.
Not armored.
Not diluted.

Known.

Deeply known.

To be known by your soul,
you must stop auditioning.

To be known by your soul,
you must let someone see what steadies you,
not just what impresses you.

To be known by your soul,
you must resist the urge to shrink to remain liked.

To be known by your soul,
you must first be honest with yourself.

A Prayer for Alignment and Justice

Father,

You see what I have seen. You know what was vowed.
You know what was violated.

I will not accuse myself for another's treachery.
Search me where I must grow,
but do not let me carry guilt that is not mine.

Judge rightly between us. Expose what is false.
Preserve what is true.

Guard my heart from bitterness.
Guard my mouth from speaking out of wound.
Guard my children from inheriting pain.

Provide what I cannot manufacture.
Stabilize what has been shaken.
Strengthen what must endure.

If there is repentance, let it be real and lasting.
If there is exposure, let it be just.
If there is separation, let it be clean.

Untangle what was counterfeit.
Seal what was covenant.
And restore my soul to wholeness before You.

You are the righteous Judge.
You are the faithful Keeper.
You are the One who never leaves nor forsakes.

In the Name of Jesus, Amen.

Warfare

Now for my warriors, intercessors and prophets: warfare prayer points.

1. Lord have Mercy on me, a sinner. If I am none of yours give me a Godly sorrow for my sins and a repentant heart and make me one of yours.

2. Holy Spirit help me in these prayers, in the Name of Jesus.

3. Father, please forgive me if I have been foolish or angry or have torn down my own house with my own hands. Forgive me, in the Name of Jesus.

4. Restore my mind and heart to right thinking and right understanding and right relationship with You and with those who I believe should never have left me if I find myself alone, in the Name of Jesus.

5. Lord, if possible, give me a way to apologize to them, and give them a heart to forgive me, for their sake as well as mine, and not solely for my own benefit, in the Name of Jesus.

6. I bind any and all outside negative interference in my relationships from known and unknown people and sources. Lord, break the source of their power to interfere with me and my life, in the Name of Jesus.

7. Lord, I close and seal any and all access openings in my life from unwanted evil interference, in Jesus' Name.

8. Lord, heal my heart, restore my soul. I bind and cast away all anger, unforgiveness, evil thoughts, evil imaginations and all works of the flesh, in the Name of Jesus.

9. Lord, have Mercy on me and deal with those that are dealing unrighteously with me, in the Name of Jesus.

10. Lord, contend with those who are contending with me. Arise Lord, and contend with them that are inflicting evil against me, whether I know them or not, in Jesus' Name.

11. Separate all evildoers against me from their source of power and render them weak and helpless to do further harm, in the Name of Jesus.

12. I bind and cast off all reproach, all evil imaginations, all lies and petty gossip about me; I am who You say I am and not who the evil doers say I am, in Jesus' Name.

13. Open the eyes of those who left me without cause. Yet I know in You I am never alone, in the Name of Jesus.

14. You said in Your Word you will never leave me or forsake me, and I believe You, Lord.

15. Blot out any evil mark on my spirit, soul or body placed by workers of iniquity; blot them out with the Blood of Jesus. I am in Christ. Amen.

16. If my smell has been tampered with, Lord wash away every evil smell by the washing of the water, by the Word. Lord, have the wind of God come and blow away any stench or evil aroma, no matter how it got on me. Blow it back to its sender, in the Name of Jesus.

17. Father, if I am looking lackluster because of stolen Glory, rebuke the thief and cause them to let go of

my glory; return my glory to me, in the Name of Jesus.

18. My star: I command any hand pointing to, an eye, eyeing my star, any obstacle hiding my star, anyone who has put my star out of course to be withered and made blind, and return my star to me, in the Name of Jesus.

19. Lord, loose my captured Star if it has been captured, in Jesus' Name.

20. I bind and remove any *spirits* of dishonor, disrespect, low esteem and low regard as it pertains to me, in the Name of Jesus

21. Lord, I repent of and I renounce all sins against You, that brought iniquity on me, in the Name of Jesus.

22. Remove all iniquity from me and my bloodline going all the way back to Adam and Eve, in the Name of Jesus.

23. *Spirit spouse*, husband of the night, wife of the night, incubus, succubus, Lilith – any evil entity that comes to promote defilement against me while I am at rest... Any entity that creates sleep paralysis to assault me sexually and cause defilement: I hate you with perfect hate. I do not

want you or anything you have. I destroy every evidence, real or fabricated of a marriage with me no matter the source or when it came into being, in the Name of Jesus.

24. Lord, destroy *spirit spouse*, it must be destroyed, in Jesus' Name.

25. I rebuke any astral projecting evil human agent or other entity that approaches me at any time in any way for any reason, especially sexual defilement. Lord, I ask you to pull their silver cord and keep them away from me forever, in the Name of Jesus.

26. Strange woman, Strange man, the Lord Jesus rebuke you. I break your charm, your evil anointing, your pull on my spouse or other beloved, in the Name of Jesus. I render you powerless against our covenant and our relationship, in the Name of Jesus.

27. *Spirit of abandonment*, *worthlessness*, *spirit* to put me away, I break your power, I break your power, and I send you now into the abyss where there is no water and no return, in the Name of Jesus.

28. *Spirit of shame*, I bind you and cast you out, in the Name of Jesus.

29. If I must go through, Lord, help me. Help me to go through peacefully, gracefully and in full strength. In the Name of Jesus.

30. Lord, show me Your Mercy and the outcome that you desire for me when this is all over, in the Name of Jesus.

31. Lord do not let my face be foul with weeping. Do not let my eyelids be dark with death, (Job 16:16), in the Name of Jesus.

32. As for he who did this to me, Lord, deal with them. Father, You see my tears, know my heart, deal according to Your Word, Your Will and Your Way, in the Name of Jesus.

33. Lord let me go through gracefully, in Jesus' Name.

34. Let me remain in godliness, in the Name of Jesus.

35. Lord, heal my heart and restore my soul, in Jesus' Name.

36. Lord, redeem the time, restore the years, in the Name of Jesus..

37. Lord, return to me the fruit of all my labor, in Jesus' Name.

38. Lord, restore relationships that should be restored; give me discernment to know, in Jesus' Name.

39. I break every evil soul tie that does not honor You and does not serve me, in Jesus' Name.

40. Lord, send Your Angel to undo all evil entanglements and let me be set free by the Son so I will be free indeed, in Jesus Name.

41. Spirit of love, power and a sound mind, come upon me now, in Jesus' Name.

42. Spirit of respect and high esteem, come upon me now, in the Name of Jesus.

43. Spirit of purpose come upon me now; Lord empower me to keep doing Your Will in the Name of Jesus.

44. Lord, thank you for my flowers now, although whomever left me may not have wanted me to have flowers—the Earth is the Lord's and the fulness thereof, in the Name of Jesus.

45. Father, let my work efforts and life not be in vain but let them show forth much fruit and fruit that remains, in the Name of Jesus.

46. Lord, call me Beulah; let me no more be forsaken. You are my helper, I will not be afraid of what man can do to me, in the Name of Jesus.

47. Lord, call me found and not lost.

48. Lord, call me remembered and not forgotten.

49. Lord, call me loved and not hated.

50. Lord, call me cherished and not disrespected.

51. Lord, call me a fruitful vine and not desolate.

52. Lord, call me blessed and highly favored,

53. In the Name of Jesus. **AMEN.**

A Closing Declaration

Scripture makes these declarations:

You are not forgotten because your strength has faded. You are not forsaken because others failed. You are not invisible because your usefulness changed.

God sees.
God remembers.
God defends.

Those who abandon what God values will answer—not to culture, not to preference, but to Him.

This book was written to leave you with clarity and Truth. It does not ask you to shrink yourself to remain loved. It asks the world to remember what covenant demands.

You were never disposable. You were never invisible. You were never forgotten by God.

Not forsaken.
Not forgotten.

- Love is not seasonal

- Covenant survives time
- Aging is not erasure
- Faithfulness still moves

God answers the lie, "Nothing beautiful remains."

A faithful man, who can find? A faithful woman, who can find?

God is the Ancient of Days, is He too old? He is the Ancient of Days. He's been here since before Time and He is older than dirt, because He made dirt. There is nothing wrong with dirt. God made the whole Earth and the fulness of it as well as all of Creation. Would we be so foolish as to leave Him because He has white hair and is ancient? Especially considering all he has done for us? God who is El Shaddai, the many breasted One, as well as the creator and director of the womb of the morning. Shall we not continue to want the blessings of the *breasts* and the *womb*?

Epilogue

You Are Not Disposable.

Dear Reader

Thank you for acquiring and reading this book, I pray it has blessed you.

Shalom,

Dr. Marlene Miles

I seal this book, all words, decrees, declarations and prayers herein across every realm, age, era, dimension, and timeline, past present and future and to infinity. I seal them with the Blood of Jesus and the Holy Spirit of Promise.

Let every retaliation against this word, these prayers, these decrees and declarations spoken, prayed, or said by the speaker, or heard by the listener, or anyone praying these words backfire without Mercy, to infinity against the evil perpetrator, in the Name of Jesus. **Amen.**

If you enjoyed this book, here are some new releases by this author.

Christ of God (*The*) 3-book series

Christ of God, (*The*) Box Set, includes all three books

Books on authority:

Authority, The Intangibles

Prayerbooks by this author

There are some books that are only prayers. You just open up the book and pray.

Prayers Against Barrenness: *For Success in Business and Life*

Fruit of the Womb: *Prayers Against Barrenness*

Beauty Curses, *Warfare Prayers Against*
https://a.co/d/5Xlc20M

Courts of Marriage: Prayers for Marriage in the Courts of Heaven *(prayerbook)* https://a.co/d/cNAdgAq

Courtroom Warfare @ Midnight *(prayerbook)* https://a.co/d/5fc7Qdp

Demonic Cobwebs *(prayerbook)* https://a.co/d/fp9Oa2H

Every Evil Bird https://a.co/d/hF1kh1O

Gates of Thanksgiving

Spirits of Death, Hell & the Grave, Pass Over Me and My House

Throne of Grace: Courtroom Prayer

Warfare Prayer Against Poverty https://a.co/d/bZ61lYu

Prayer Manuals

FAKE FRIENDS: *Prayers Against Betrayers*

HOLIDAY WARFARE Prayer Manual (humorous) Surviving Family Gatherings All Year Long (without catching a case)

SOUL TIE Prayer Manual (The) Part of a 3-part series including a workbook.

MAD at DADDY Prayer Manual – part of a 3-part series including a workbook.

Healing the Sibling & Relative Wound Prayer Manual

Healing the Father-Son Wound Prayer Manual

Prayers Against Barrenness: *For Success in Business and Life*

Breaking Curses of the Mother Prayer Manual

Other books by this author

Abundance of Jesus (The) https://a.co/d/5gHJVed

AK: The Adventures of the Agape Kid

Already Married in the Spirit: *Why You May Not Be Married in the Natural*

AMONG SOME THIEVES https://a.co/d/dkYT4ZV

Ancestral Powers

Anti-Marriage, *The Spirit of*

Backstabbers https://a.co/d/gi8iBxf

Barrenness, *Prayers Against* https://a.co/d/feUltIs

Battlefield of Marriage, *The*

Beware of the Dog: Prayers Against Dogs in the Dream.

Bless Your Food: *Let the Dining Table be Undefiled* *https://a.co/d/6oPMRDv*

Blindsided: *Has the Old Man Bewitched You?* https://a.co/d/5O2fLLR

Break Free from Collective Captivity

Broken Spirits & Dry Bones

By Means of a Whorish Father

Caged Life: Get Out Alive! https://a.co/d/bwPbksX

Casting Down Imaginations

Christ of God (*The*) 3-book series

Christ of God, (*The*) Box Set, includes all three books

Churchzilla, The Wanna-Be, Supposed-to-be Bride of Christ https://a.co/d/eAf5j3x

Collateral Damage: *When What Happened Spiritually Was Your Fault*

Demonic Cobwebs (prayerbook)

Demonic Time Bombs

Demons Hate Questions

Devil Loves Trauma, *The*

Devil Weapons: Unforgiveness, Bitterness,...

The Devourers: Thieves of Darkness 2

Do Not Swear by the Moon

Don't Refuse Me, Lord (4 book series)

https://a.co/d/idP34LG

Dream Defilement

The Emptiers: *Thieves of Darkness, 1* https://a.co/d/5I4n5mc

Entanglements: *Illegal Knots Limiting Your Life*

Evil Touch

Failed Assignment

Fantasy Spirit Spouse https://a.co/d/hW7oYbX

FAT Demons (The): *Breaking Demonic Curses* https://a.co/d/4kP8wV1

The Fold (5-book series)

- The Fold (Book 1)
- Name Your Seed (Book 2)
- The Poor Attitudes of Money (3)
- Do Not Orphan Your Seed (4)
- For the Sake of the Gospel (5)
- My Sowing Journal

Gang Ups: Touch Not God's Anointed

Gathered: No Longer Scattered https://a.co/d/1i5DPIX

Getting Rid of Evil Spiritual Food

https://a.co/d/i2L3WYQ

got HEALING? Verses for Life

got LOVE? Verses for Life https://a.co/d/8seXHPd

got HOPE? Verses for Life

got money? https://a.co/d/g2av41N

100 Green Flags: Date This Not That *& Workbook*

Has My Soul Been Sold? https://a.co/d/dyB8hhA

Here Come the Horns: *Skilled to Destroy* https://a.co/d/cZiNnkP

Hidden Sins: Hidden Iniquity

https://a.co/d/4Mth0wa

How A Man Is Owned

How to Dental Assist

How to Dental Assist2: Be Productive, Not Wasteful

How To Stay Prayed Up

How to STOP Being a Blind Witch or Warlock

I Take It Back

In Multiplying I Will Multiply Thee

Intangibles (*The*)

Into Freedom:

Irresistible: Jesus' Triumphal Entry
https://a.co/d/d09IfEC

KNOW YOUR BATTLE: Stop Swinging Blindly — and Win Against Opponents, Adversaries & Enemies (Workbook) https://a.co/d/eOwFKlV

Legacy

Let Me Have A Dollar's Worth
https://a.co/d/h8F8XgE

Level the Playing Field

Living for the NOW of God
https://a.co/d/6bK5duE

Lose My Location https://a.co/d/crD6mV9

Love Breaks Your Heart

Mad At Daddy: Healing Father-Wounds that Affect Motherhood (book, workbook & prayer manual)

Made Perfect In Love

Mammon https://a.co/d/29yhMG7

Man Safari, *The*

Marriage Ed.: *Rules of Engagement & Marriage*

Made Perfect in Love

Money Hunters: Beware of Those

Money on the Altar https://a.co/d/4EqJ2Nr

Mulberry Tree, *The* https://a.co/d/9nR9rRb

Motherboard (The)- *Soul Prosperity Series*

Name Your Seed

Not Forsaken Or Forgotten

Occupy: ***Until I Return*** https://a.co/d/bZ7ztUy

One Defining Day: ***A Day When Dreams Come True***

Opponent, Adversary, or Enemy?: Fight The Right Battle with the Right Weapons

https://a.co/d/byQqEE2 & companion workbook: Know Your Battle

Plantation Souls

Players Gonna Play

Portals: Shut the Front Door: Prayers to Close Evil Portals.

Power Money: Nine Times the Tithe

https://a.co/d/gRt41gy

The Power to Get Wealth https://a.co/d/e4ub4Ov

Powers Above

The Robe, Part 1, The Lessons of Joseph

The Robe, Part II, The Lessons of Joseph

Seasons of Grief

Seasons of Siege: God Is Coming

Seasons of Waiting

Seasons of War

Second Marriage, Third--, *Any Marriage*

https://a.co/d/6m6GN4N

Seducing Spirits: Idolatry & Whoredoms

https://a.co/d/4Jq4WEs

Shut the Front Door: *Prayers to Close Portals* https://a.co/d/cH4TWJj

Siege: *God Is Coming*

Sift You Like Wheat

Silences of God (*The)*

Six Men Short: What Has Happened to all the Men?

SLAVE

Sleep Afflictions & Really Bad Dreams https://a.co/d/f8sDmgv

Soul Prosperity soul prosperity series 3

https://a.co/d/5p8YvCN

Soul Ties: How Soul Ties Form, and How To Break Them (book, workbook & prayer manual)

Souls In Captivity

The Spirit of Anti-Marriage

The Spirit of Poverty https://a.co/d/abV2o2e

Spiritual Thieves https://a.co/d/eqPPz33

StarStruck- Triangular Power series.

SUNBLOCK- Triangular Power series.

The Swallowers: *Thieves of Darkness,* 3

Take It Back

This Is NOT That: How to Keep Demons from Coming at You

THRONES: Not A Game

Time Is of the Essence

Too Many Wives: *Why You Have Lady Problems*

Tormenting Spirits https://a.co/d/dAogEJf

Toxic Souls

Tribe: *What Covenants Are Governing You…?*

Triangular Power *(series),* Powers Above, SUNBLOCK, Do Not Swear by the Moon, STARSTRUCK

TRIBE: *What Covenants Are Governing You…?*

Unbreak My Heart: *Don't Let Me Die*

Uncontested Doom

Ungovered Hunger: How Unchecked Appetite Dismantles Authority

Unguarded Hours, *The*

Unseen Life, *The* (forthcoming)

Upgrade: How to Get Out of Survival Mode Toxic Souls (Book 2 of series) , Legacy (Book 3 of series)

The Wasters: *Thieves of Darkness*, Bk 2 https://a.co/d/bUvI9Jo

What Have You to Declare? What Do You Have With You from Where You've Been?

When I Was A Child, *I Prayed As a Child*

When the Devourer is Rebuked https://a.co/d/1HVv8oq

When The Table Is Set Against You

WTH? Get Me Out of This Hell https://a.co/d/a7WBGJh

The Wilderness Romance *(series)* is about conducting a Godly relationship and marriage with someone who is a Wilderness person. *The Social Wilderness*

- *The Sexual Wilderness*
- *The Spiritual Wilderness*

Other Series

The Fold (a series on Godly finances) https://a.co/d/4hz3unj

Soul Prosperity Series https://a.co/d/bz2M42q

Spirit Spouse books

https://a.co/d/9VehDSo

https://a.co/d/97sKOwm

Battlefield of Marriage, The

https://a.co/d/eUDzizO

Players Gonna Play

https://a.co/d/2hzGw3N

Sent Spirit Spouse (can someone send you a spirit spouse? This book is not yet released.)

Matters of the Heart, Made Perfect in Love

https://a.co/d/70MQW3O , Love Breaks Your Heart https://a.co/d/4KvuQLZ, Unbreak My Heart https://a.co/d/84ceZ6M Broken Spirits & Dry Bones https://a.co/d/e6iedNP

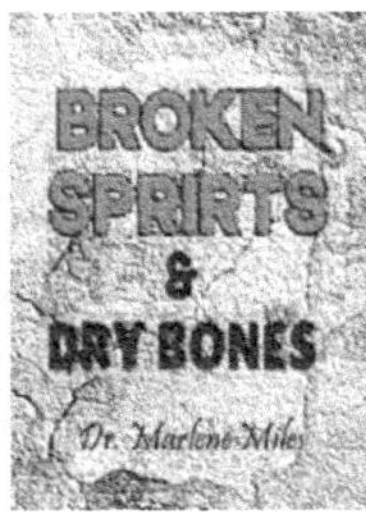

Thieves of Darkness series

The Emptiers https://a.co/d/heioOdO

The Wasters https://a.co/d/5TG1iNQ

The Swallowers https://a.co/d/1jWhM6G

The Devourers: Why We Can't Have Nice Things https://a.co/d/87Tejbf

Spiritual Thieves

Red Flags: The Track Is Not Safe (book & workbook)

Triangular Powers https://a.co/d/aUCjAWC

Upgrade (series) *How to Get Out of Survival Mode* https://a.co/d/aTERhXO

We Get Along, Right? Compatibility for Couples – (book & workbook)

The **100 Green Flags Book: Date This Not That and the companion Workbook, DATE THIS NOT THAT WORKBOOK**

Dr. Marlene Miles is a teacher, author, and spiritual thinker known for her grounded, discerning approach to prayer and spiritual formation. Her work emphasizes clarity, restraint, and maturity in faith—helping believers move beyond emotionalism and performance into a steady, practiced walk with God.

With a deep respect for Scripture and a practical understanding of daily life, Dr. Miles writes for those who want their prayer life to be formed, not dramatized. Her teaching encourages spiritual maintenance, discernment, and responsibility—so faith remains strong not only in crisis, but in everyday living.

www.ingramcontent.com/pod-product-compliance
Lightning Source LLC
LaVergne TN
LVHW010948110826
845149LV00015B/3253
* 9 7 8 1 9 7 1 9 3 3 3 5 1 *